GREAT SMOKY MOUNTAINS NATIONAL PARK

DEBORAH HUSO

Contents

Cherokee Indian Reservation and Maggie Valley 8

Planning Your Time. 9

Maggie Valley 11

Sights 11
Ghost Town in the Sky 11
Wheels Through Time
    Motorcycle Museum. 11

Entertainment and Events 11
Entertainment. 11
Events. 12

Sports and Recreation 12
Skiing and Snowmobiling 12

Accommodations. 12

Food. 14

Information and Services. 14
Information 14
Emergency Services. 14
Post Office. 14

Getting There 14

Cherokee 14

Sights 15
[C] Museum of the Cherokee Indian .. 15
Oconaluftee Indian Village 16

Shopping 17
[C] Qualla Arts and Crafts Mutual 17
Other Shops 18

Entertainment and Events 18
[C] Harrah's Casino 18

[C] Unto These Hills 18
Festivals. 19

Sports and Recreation 19
Hiking. 19
[C] Mingo Falls. 19
Fishing 20
Golf. 20

Accommodations. 20

Food. 21

Information and Services. 22
Information 22
Emergency Services. 22

Getting There and Around 22
Car 22
Public Transportation 22

Bryson City. 23

Sights 23
Great Smoky Mountains
    Railroad 23

Shopping 23

Entertainment and Events 24
Singing in the Smokies 24

Sports and Recreation 24
Rafting and Tubing. 24
Zip Line 25

Accommodations. 25

Food. 25

Information and Services. 26
Information 26
Emergency Services. 26
Post Office. 26

Getting There 26

Great Smoky Mountains National Park 27

Planning Your Time..............28

Exploring the Park 30

Visitors Centers.................30
Oconaluftee Visitor Center..........30
Sugarlands Visitor Center
 and Park Headquarters..........30
Cades Cove Visitor Center 31

Programs 31
Park Ranger Programs 31
Junior Ranger Program............31
Smoky Mountain Field School 31

Entrance Stations...............32

Driving Tours....................32
◖ Newfound Gap Road 32
◖ Roaring Fork Motor
 Nature Trail....................34
◖ Cades Cove 34

Newfound Gap Road..........37

Sights...........................37
Oconaluftee Visitor Center
 and Mountain Farm Museum 37
Mingus Mill.......................38
Webb Overlook 38
Deep Creek Valley Overlook........38
Oconaluftee River Valley Overlook ...38
◖ Clingmans Dome...............39
Newfound Gap....................39
Morton Overlook..................39
River Pull-Offs....................39
Campbell Overlook................39
Sugarlands Visitor Center..........40

Hiking...........................40
Clingmans Dome..................40
◖ Alum Cave Bluffs Trail........... 41

Horseback Riding................42

Camping.........................43

Picnicking.......................43
Collins Creek Picnic Area...........43
Chimneys Picnic Area 43

Roaring Fork and Greenbrier Cove............43

Roaring Fork 44
Sights...........................44
Hiking...........................45

Greenbrier Cove..................48
Horseback Riding..................48
Hiking...........................48

Little River Road..............49

Sights...........................49
Elkmont 49
Great Smoky Mountains
 Institute at Tremont.............50

Hiking...........................50
Laurel Falls 50

Camping.........................50

Cades Cove 51

Sights...........................54
John Oliver Place.................54
Methodist Church.................54
Cable Mill Historic Area............54
Tipton Place......................55

Biking 55

Horseback Riding................55

**Scenic Drives and
 Motorcycle Tours** 56
Parson Branch Road 56
Deals Gap.......................57

Camping.........................57

Fontana Lake Area 58
[Fontana Dam 58
Fontana Marina...................59
Fontana Village...................59
  Resort............................59
  Camping..........................59

Deep Creek.....................60
Hiking............................60
  Juney Whank Falls 60
  Indian Creek Falls 60
Road to Nowhere 60
Camping..........................60

**Cataloochee Valley
and Balsam Mountain** 61
Sights.............................62
  Palmer Chapel and Cemetery.......62
  Beech Grove School................63
  Caldwell House 63
  Palmer House 63
Scenic Drives.....................64
  Balsam Mountain Road 64
Hiking............................65
  Woody Place 65
Camping...........................66

Practicalities..................67
Information 67
Emergency Services 67
Getting There 67

Tennessee Foothills....68
Planning Your Time...............69

Gatlinburg 71

Sights.............................71
[Arrowmont School of
  Arts and Crafts.................. 71
Ripley's Aquarium of the Smokies....73
Gatlinburg Sky Lift 73
Space Needle......................73
Shopping 73
[Great Smoky Arts and Crafts
  Community......................73
  The Village.......................75
  Downtown Galleries 75
  Downtown Gifts...................76
Entertainment and Events 76
  Annual Wildflower Pilgrimage 76
  Gatlinburg Fine Arts Festival 76
  Gatlinburg Craftsmen's Fair 76
  Gatlinburg Winter Magic 76
Sports and Recreation 76
[Ober Gatlinburg 76
  White-Water Rafting...............77
  Zip Line 77
  Hummer Tours 78
Accommodations.................78
Food.............................82
Information and Services.........83
  Information 83
  Emergency Services...............83
  Media 83
Getting There 84
Getting Around...................84
  Parking..........................84
  Gatlinburg Trolley System..........84

Pigeon Forge and
Sevierville....................85
Sights.............................85
[Dollywood 85
  Dollywood's Splash Country........88
  Titanic Pigeon Forge 89
  Tennessee Museum of Aviation 89

Dolly Parton Statue 89

Shopping 89
🄲 Old Mill Square 89
Specialty Stores 90

Entertainment and Events 90
Entertainment .90
Events 91

Sports and Recreation 92
Zorb 92
Indoor Skydiving 92
Helicopter Tours 92
Golf 92

Accommodations 92

Food 94

Information and Services 95
Information 95
Emergency Services 95

Getting There .96
Getting Around 96

Townsend 96

Sights 96
Tuckaleechee Caverns 96
Great Smoky Mountains
Heritage Center 96
Foothills Parkway 96

Sports and Recreation 97
Horseback Riding 97
Tours 97

Accommodations 97

Food 98

Information and Services 99

Getting There .99

GREAT SMOKY MOUNTAINS NATIONAL PARK

CHEROKEE INDIAN RESERVATION AND MAGGIE VALLEY

The North Carolina entry point to the Great Smoky Mountains National Park, the Cherokee Indian Reservation, is home to the Eastern Band of the Cherokee Nation, the descendants of those who avoided the Trail of Tears to the Oklahoma Territory in 1838, or those who returned years later. Tourism has brought prosperity to the town of Cherokee as well as the nearby off-reservation town of Maggie Valley. The Museum of the Cherokee Indian is a must-see starting point to understanding the long history and culture of the tribe, and many galleries and shops in town offer the opportunity to purchase locally made Cherokee crafts. Of course, tourism has also brought some of the glitz more reminiscent of the western side of the Smokies, including the palatial Harrah's Casino. The benefit, however, is that the casino regularly hosts big-name artists like Miranda Lambert and George Jones.

Just south of Cherokee is a venue for those seeking quiet, the small town of Bryson City, where one can stay overnight at one of many small bed-and-breakfasts or hop aboard the Great Smoky Mountains Railroad for scenic trips through the mountains. To the north of Cherokee and accessible via winding Highway 19 is the strip town of Maggie Valley. Stretching for miles on either side of the highway through what would otherwise be a scenic mountain valley, Maggie Valley is mostly a whirlwind of motels, miniature golf courses, theaters, and tourist traps. It is perhaps the attempt of the North Carolina side of the Smokies to answer the hoopla of Tennessee's Pigeon Forge, though on a much smaller scale.

HIGHLIGHTS

◖ **Museum of the Cherokee Indian:** This beautifully done museum offers the history and artifacts of the Cherokee from ancient times to the present (page 15).

◖ **Qualla Arts and Crafts Mutual:** The oldest Native American craft cooperative in the country showcases and sells locally made Cherokee crafts (page 17).

◖ **Harrah's Casino:** The Cherokee-owned casino offers big-name shows and 24-hour gaming that financially supports the community initiatives of the Eastern Band of the Cherokee (page 18).

◖ **Unto These Hills:** This summer outdoor drama tells the story of the Cherokee removal from North Carolina (page 18).

◖ **Mingo Falls:** Cascading over 120 feet, this lovely waterfall is just outside the town of Cherokee and accessible via a quick hike (page 19).

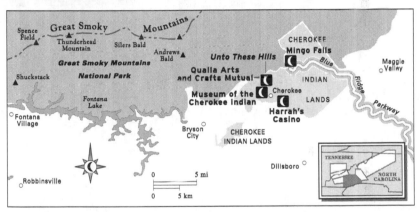

LOOK FOR ◖ TO FIND RECOMMENDED SIGHTS, ACTIVITIES, DINING, AND LODGING.

PLANNING YOUR TIME

Allow yourself at least one full day in Cherokee so you have time to fully explore the highlights that will give you a grounding in the region's Native American history. Those include the Museum of the Cherokee Indian, the Oconaluftee Indian Village, Qualla Arts and Crafts Mutual, and the outdoor drama *Unto These Hills*. A second day will give you time to either hit some of the amusements of nearby Maggie Valley, like Ghost Town in the Sky, or to explore the village of Bryson City and ride the Great Smoky Mountains Railroad.

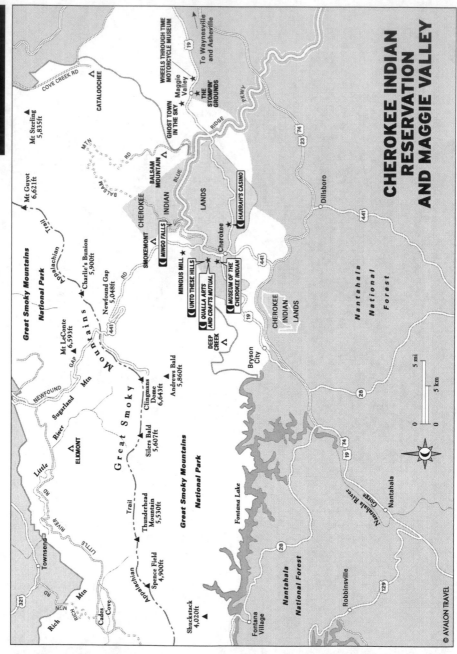

CHEROKEE INDIAN
RESERVATION
AND MAGGIE VALLEY

© AVALON TRAVEL

Maggie Valley

More strip than town, Maggie Valley is one of the eastern gateways into the Smokies, the last town before entering the Cherokee Indian Reservation and Great Smoky Mountains National Park. Many of the attractions are hokey at best, but there are some genuinely good clogging shows here as well as an annual motorcycle festival (and Harley rentals!).

Maggie Valley is located on the western edge of Haywood County, which claims to have the highest average elevation of any county in the East with 13 peaks rising over 6,000 feet.

SIGHTS
Ghost Town in the Sky

Ghost Town in the Sky (16 Fie Top Rd., 828/926-1140, www.ghosttowninthesky.com, May Fri.–Mon. 10 A.M.–6 P.M., June–mid-Sept. daily 10 A.M.–6 P.M., mid-Sept.–Oct. Fri.–Sun. 10 A.M.–6 P.M., adults $29.95, children $24.95) has been a part of the attraction scene in Maggie Valley for half a century, quite a claim for an amusement park. But that's not even the biggest news about this place: Even more remarkable is that the cowboy who plays the Apache Kid has served in the role since the 1960s.

Even if you enjoy the thrilling rides of amusement parks, Ghost Town in the Sky may come across as a bit cheesy with its Wild West theme in the middle of the Smoky Mountains, but keep your judgment in check and just enjoy the rides, which include the Cliff Hanger roller coaster. As its name suggests, this ride clings to the side of Buck Mountain, offering incredible views if you're brave enough to enjoy them.

Any visit to Ghost Town in the Sky begins with a 15-minute chairlift ride up the mountain since the 90-acre amusement park is situated at 4,000 feet. The park has rides for all ages and thrill-seeker levels as well as shoot-outs, cancan girls, tribal dancing, bluegrass bands, and a saloon.

Wheels Through Time Motorcycle Museum

Wheels Through Time Motorcycle Museum (2914 Soco Rd., 828/926 6266, www.wheelsthroughtime.com, daily 9 A.M.–5 P.M., adults $12, seniors $10, children $6, group rate for six or more $10 each) is a draw for the motorcyclists that flock to the Smokies for great rides through the mountains. Unbelievably, it draws some half a million visitors a year, who come to see their favorite machines on two wheels displayed in historical review. The museum also hosts regular openings and exhibitions throughout the year with even more bikes to check out. Visit the website for days and times.

ENTERTAINMENT AND EVENTS
Entertainment

Maggie Valley is known for its musical entertainment, and there are more than half a dozen venues in town where you can enjoy live music. The best among them is **Carolina Nights** (3732 Soco Rd., 828/926-8822, www.maggievalleyusa.com, showtime 6:15–9 P.M., $29.95 dinner, show, and all taxes), a dinner theater that presents one major musical show a year and, despite the theater's location in the Appalachian Mountains, the genres you'll enjoy here will not necessarily be country. Dinners are served cafeteria-style.

The Stompin' Grounds (3116 Soco Rd., 828/926-1288) holds a Clogging Competition the first weekend in May, and the American Clogging Hall of Fame World Championships is held on the fourth Saturday in October. The Stompin' Grounds is home to the American Clogging Hall of Fame, which honors America's clogging history and the cloggers of today. The public is always welcome to attend the competitions here—and should. If you think clogging is a hokey mountain dance done by old ladies in puffy skirts, then you need to check

the Apache Kid at Ghost Town in the Sky

this place out. You've never seen clogging like this before.

Events

Thunder in the Smokies (3374 Soco Rd., 828/246-2101, www.handlebarcorral.com, $15) is a motorcycle rally held each year in both April and September with organized rides through the countryside, live music, including gospel on Sunday, vendors, and bike games. Thousands of bikers attend every year and take rides together on the Parkway, into Asheville, and into Cherokee. **Gryphon Bikes** (871 Soco Rd., 828/926-4400, www.gryphonbikes.com, daily rental $109–215, 3-day rental $294–429, 5-day rental $465–675) offers Harley rentals by the day if you don't have your own bike.

SPORTS AND RECREATION
Skiing and Snowmobiling

The **Cataloochee Ski Area** (1080 Ski Lodge Rd., 800/768-0285, www.cataloochee.com, Nov.–Mar. hours vary, lift tickets $33–53, equipment rental $20–23) has 16 slopes and trails open to skiers and snowboarders as well

as Tube World (www.tubemaggievalley.com, $25) with a mechanical tow to the top. Ski lessons and rentals are available. Even the chairlift rides here are fun, as they offer a chance to sit back and enjoy the long-distance Smoky Mountain views. There are 50 skiable acres; the top elevation is 5,400 feet, with a vertical drop of 740 feet. For ski reports, call 800/768-3588.

ACCOMMODATIONS
Hotels

Maggie Valley is loaded with hotels and motels of all descriptions, many of them 1950s-style motor inns. If you're looking for accommodations with more amenities and more plush surroundings, you might prefer to stay at an inn or bed-and-breakfast in the neighboring town of Waynesville or stay in a vacation rental. Your best bet for hotels, at least in Maggie Valley, is more likely a chain option. That being said, there are a few locally owned hotels that provide more updated overnight lodgings. Among them is the **Jonathan Creek Inn** (4324 Soco Rd., 800/577-7812, www.jonathancreekinn.com, standard rooms $50–110, creek rooms $65–125, rooms with hot tub and fireplace $75–150, villas $150–395), which has a mixture of lodging options available, including creekside rooms, rooms with whirlpool baths, rooms with hot tubs, and even villas. All are comfortably if simply furnished and offer a peaceful setting in the midst of town. Guests have use of the hotel's indoor heated pool, a creekside hot tub, game room, stocked trout stream, Internet station in the lobby, and free Wi-Fi.

Smoky Falls Lodge (2550 Soco Rd., 877/926-7440, www.smokyfallslodge.com, standard rooms $89, larger rooms with fireplaces $109–199, 3-bedroom apartment $229) is another private option on the main drag in Maggie Valley. With creekside rooms, many with fireplaces, and cozy, rustic furnishings, this hotel option is more peaceful than it appears from the street. All guests enjoy complimentary Wi-Fi, and the lodge is motorcycle friendly, offering covered parking for bikers. The Grizzly Grill offers dining on-site.

Best Western Mountainbrook Inn (3811 Soco Rd., 800/213-1914, www.bestwestern.com/mountainbrookinn, $80–159) offers 50 rooms, all with microwave, fridge, and coffee maker as well as free Wi-Fi. Guests enjoy complimentary continental breakfast each morning as well as access to an outdoor pool and indoor spa. The **Comfort Inn** (3282 Soco Rd., 866/926-9106, www.comfortinnmaggie.com, $49–269) has 68 rooms with microwaves, fridges, and high-speed Internet access. Some hot-tub rooms are available, too. Guests can enjoy the hotel's indoor pool or take a break in one of the rocking chairs in the hotel gazebo.

The **Ramada Limited** (4048 Soco Rd., 800/305-6703, www.ramada.com, $115–213) has creekside rooms with private balconies if you're interested in a little more than the standard hotel atmosphere. The hotel has whirlpool and family suites available as well as microwaves and refrigerators in each room. Guests enjoy use of the indoor heated pool and hot tub and complimentary continental breakfast each morning.

Cabins

Boyd Mountain Log Cabins & Christmas Tree Farm (445 Boyd Farm Rd., 828/926-1575, www.boydmountain.com, $165–385) offers overnight accommodations in restored antique log cabins on a 130-acre Christmas tree farm. The cabins are on the rustic side but are fully equipped with kitchens and everything you need to set up housekeeping for a couple of days. One-, two-, and three-bedroom cabins are available, and all feature covered porches with rocking chairs for taking in the views. There is also on-site fishing available on three stocked ponds and a stream.

Equestrian lovers might consider staying at **Cataloochee Ranch** (119 Ranch Dr., 800/868-1401, www.cataloocheeranch.com, main ranch house $152–215, Silverbell Lodge $205–247, cabins $247–268, romance cabins $320, 2- and 3-bedroom cabins $446), which has a variety of rustic log cabins available for rent as well as lodge rooms. Accommodations are simple and sparse but comfortable with many cabins offering fireplaces and decks with lovely views. Half- and full-day horseback riding is available for ranch guests and non-guests with rates starting at $45 for guests. Breakfast and dinner are included in the room and cabin rates.

Camping

Creekwood Farm RV Park (4696 Jonathan Creek Rd., 800/862-8110, www.creekwoodfarmrv.com, $30–48) has 125 sites, some on the river, and all with full hookups. Sites also have access to cable TV hookups.

Stone Bridge RV Resort (1786 Soco Rd., 828/926-1904, www.stonebridgervresort.com, $25–42) has 300 campsites for tents and RVs. In addition to full hookups this luxurious campground has Wi-Fi, cable TV, three bathhouses, laundry facilities, 46 campsites on a stocked trout creek, basketball courts, horseshoe pits, an arcade, dump station, and firewood and ice available on-site.

Rippling Waters Creekside RV Park (3962 Soco Rd., 828/926-7787) is open year-round, and has laundry and bathrooms available as well as full hookups.

FOOD

Joey's Pancake House (4309 Soco Rd., 828/926-0212, www.joeyspancake.com, Fri.–Wed. 7 A.M.–noon, $4–8) is probably a standout because it's one of the few options for breakfast in Maggie Valley, and it has consistently fast and friendly service. Here you'll find omelets of all descriptions, breakfast crepes, biscuits and gravy, country ham—all the usual yummy suspects.

J. Arthur's Restaurant (2843 Soco Rd., 828/926-1817, www.jarthurs.com, May–Oct. daily 4:30–9 P.M., Nov.–Apr. Wed.–Thurs. 4:30–9 P.M., $4–28) is one of the most popular in Maggie Valley and has a huge dining room and a menu that's almost as big. While they're well appreciated for their prime ribs and steak, their gorgonzola cheese salads are the best. If you want to eat on the lighter side, J. Arthur's also has a huge salad bar served with as many warm rolls with butter as you can stand to eat.

Grizzly Grill (2550 Soco Rd., 877/926-7440, www.thegrizzlygrill.com, $5–16) is best known for its barbecue, which you can have sweet, medium, or hot on more than a few of the menu offerings, from pork and chicken plates to pulled-pork sandwiches. The restaurant also serves steaks, burgers, and pizza.

INFORMATION AND SERVICES
Information
The **Haywood County Tourism Development Authority** (1233 N. Main St., Ste. 1-40, Waynesville, 800/334-9036, www.smokeymountains.net, Mon.–Fri. 9 A.M.–5 P.M.) is in Waynesville just down the road. Take Highway 19 north, and turn right on Highway 74/23, and follow the visitors center signs to downtown.

Emergency Services
Haywood Regional Medical Center (262 Leroy George Dr., 828/456-7311, www.haymed.org, 24 hours) in neighboring Clyde offers 24-hour emergency service.

Post Office
The **Maggie Valley Post Office** (4280 Soco Rd., 828/926-0679, Mon.–Fri. 8:30 A.M.–4:30 P.M.) is located right next door to the Jonathan Creek Inn on Highway 19.

GETTING THERE
To reach Maggie Valley from the south, take I-85 north to I-985 north, which becomes Highway 365/23 north. Then follow Highway 23/441 north to Dillsboro. At Dillsboro, take Highway 23/74 east to Waynesville/Maggie Valley. Take Exit 102B for Maggie Valley. If you're coming in From Asheville, take I-40 west. Take Exit 20 for Maggie Valley. From points west, take I-40 towards Asheville, but get off the interstate at Exit 20 before reaching Asheville.

Cherokee

While Cherokee has become more famous in recent years due to the addition of a Harrah's Casino to the town, the things you really don't want to miss here include the numerous museums, villages, and galleries providing insight into the heritage and history of the Cherokee Nation. The people who live here are the descendants of those who didn't take the Trail of Tears to Oklahoma.

The southern Appalachians have been home to the Cherokee and their early ancestors for thousands of years. At its height, prior to European contact in the mid-1600s, the Cherokee Nation consisted of 36,000 people occupying 140,000 square miles of territory in eight present-day southern states.

By the mid-18th century, many Cherokee had become farmers and sent their children to white schools, and some had even converted to Christianity. Most felt they were safe from encroachment by white settlers because of King George III's Proclamation of 1763, which stated that there would be no white settlement in the Appalachian Mountains and points west. By the 1780s, however, the U.S. Civilization Policy was in full effect with the intent of assimilating all Native Americans, including the Cherokee.

Prospects for the Cherokee went from bad to worse in 1835, when Major Ridge, without full approval of the Cherokee Nation or Chief John Ross, signed the Treaty of New Echota. The treaty allowed for the sale of the Cherokee homeland to the federal government for $5 million. In addition, all Cherokee were required to abandon their homes and move west to Indian Territory. Some 16,000 Cherokee, including Chief John Ross, made the journey. Some Cherokee, however, applied to become U.S. citizens, separated from the Cherokee Nation, and occupied their own privately owned reservation, what is today known as the Qualla Boundary. The current residents of North Carolina's Cherokee Indian Reservation are the descendants of those few who managed to stay behind.

Cherokee didn't gain its place as a tourist destination until the 1950s, when the Museum of the Cherokee Indian was founded. It was at this time that tourists began to see "roadside chiefs" in Cherokee, local men dressed in popularized Indian garb including elaborate headdresses. You can still find some of these "roadside chiefs" in town, as they continue their efforts to appeal to a visitor demographic that craves the popular over the realistic.

The Qualla Boundary is a prosperous, if touristy, place loaded with gift shops, restaurants, and hotels. The reservation covers 100 square miles, and some 14,000 members of the Eastern Band of the Cherokee currently reside here.

Most visitors travel into Cherokee via Highway 19 from Maggie Valley, coming across Soco Gap, an area that is loaded with roadside fruit stands and junk shops, selling everything from boiled peanuts to overstock dishware.

SIGHTS
◖ Museum of the Cherokee Indian

The Museum of the Cherokee Indian (589 Tsali Blvd., 828/497-3481, www.cherokeemuseum. org, June–Aug. Mon.–Sat. 9 A.M.–7 P.M., Sun. 9 A.M.–5 P.M., Sept.–May daily 9 A.M.–5 P.M., adults $9, children 6–13 $6, 5 and under free) is the place you should start your exploration of the Cherokee Indian Reservation. This well-organized museum provides a good overview of the Native American history of the mountains of western North Carolina beginning with exhibits on the Paleo Indians who lived in the area during the last Ice Age. The museum traces many Cherokee traditions and crafts, including the tribe's well-known and beautiful basket weaving, to origins as early as 7500 B.C. There are many examples of woven and coiled baskets on display as well as dozens of examples of historic Cherokee pottery and effigy bowls, which are made in the shapes of humans or animals.

Among the museum's most interesting exhibits is one on Sequoyah, the only recorded historical figure to have created a complete writing system without having first been literate in another language. Sequoyah took the Cherokee's native tongue and developed a written language from it. Take a few moments to listen to the Cherokee alphabet, and see if you can follow the complex characters, each one of which stands for a syllable. Sequoyah, who was the son of a white father and a Cherokee mother, completed his writing system in 1821.

The Cherokee, in fact, developed their own newspaper in the written language that Sequoyah developed, and you can view an 1870 Cherokee printing press here as well.

The Museum of the Cherokee Indian also briefly reviews the story of William Holland Thomas, a 12-year-old white orphan who moved to the Oconaluftee River region of western North Carolina and was adopted by a Cherokee Chief called Yonaguska or Drowning Bear. Yonaguska and his people applied for U.S. citizenship under the Treaty of 1817 once they saw removal would otherwise

GROWING MATERIALS FOR ART

While the average visitor to Cherokee doesn't think about it, most of the Cherokee crafts one sees for sale in the town are made using natural local resources, from clay to oak trees. But some of the natural resources on which the Cherokee depend to make their beautiful and functional wares are fading from the landscape.

Among them is the butternut tree, which the Cherokee have used for generations as a source of both dye for baskets and textiles and wood for carving. The butternut has been subject to a blight similar to that of the American chestnut, so the local Qualla Arts and Crafts Mutual has partnered with the University of Tennessee to re-establish butternut trees on the reservation. They have developed a blight-resistant butternut and have begun planting its seedlings in the town of Kituwah with seedlings also available for locals to plant in their yards.

Local craftspeople are also encouraging their neighbors to plant river cane, which is used in the crafting of many of the beautiful Cherokee baskets you'll find at the Qualla Arts and Crafts Mutual and other shops in town. River-cane habitat has shrunk over recent decades to 2 percent of its original size, so today Cherokee artists and residents are planting the cane for a dual purpose – to supply local art and to promote soil conservation and stream restoration.

Carolina in 1866. The federal government acknowledged the Eastern Band two years later, establishing today's reservation out of lands purchased by Thomas. You can read the fictionalized version of the story in Charles Frazier's *Thirteen Moons,* which is available for purchase in the museum gift shop along with a host of other books on Cherokee history, culture, and language, including Cherokee-English dictionaries and a Cherokee-language version of *Thirteen Moons.*

The museum gift shop also sells locally made Cherokee handicrafts as well as T-shirts and souvenirs. On the lawn of the museum is an example of the Cherokee Bear Project, which features the artistry of more than a dozen local artists who have painted bears to represent the landscape, history, and heritage of the Smoky Mountains. In front of the Museum of the Cherokee Indian is "Sequoyah Syllabeary," a bear painted to resemble Sequoyah, the creator of the Cherokee alphabet.

Oconaluftee Indian Village

The Oconaluftee Indian Village (Drama Rd., 866/554-4557, May–Oct. daily 9 A.M.–5 P.M., adults $15, children 6–12 $6, 5 and under free) is located on a hillside just above the Museum of the Cherokee Indian and interprets an 18th-century Cherokee community. The outdoor living-history museum has a variety of costumed interpreters demonstrating everything from basket weaving and beadwork to finger weaving and pottery making.

The village also features a model of a partially underground sweathouse and replicas of 1700s log homes like those in which the Cherokee would have lived. The most interesting demonstration here is probably the canoe-making process, where interpreters burn out the shell of a canoe from a log with the slow but effective use of fire. Burning out the hull of a canoe in this way typically takes six months, but it saved on the backbreaking labor that would have been required of manually digging out the wood. Throughout the day interpreters hold scheduled talks on Cherokee life and customs as well as hold demonstrations of

be inevitable. Young Thomas ultimately became an attorney and advocated for Yonaguska and his tribe, even going so far as to gain them some of the funds the Cherokee received under the Treaty of New Echota. It was Yonaguska's people as well as some Cherokee who hid in the mountains and escaped removal that ultimately formed the Eastern Band of the Cherokee. They were formally recognized as their own distinct nation by the state of North

craft demonstration at Oconaluftee Indian Village in Cherokee

traditional dance and battle reenactments. The village also offers hands-on classes in pottery and basketry at the outdoor village classroom for $35 per person.

The one problem here is that the interpreters do not volunteer information on the history of their crafts or the process of their work, making the experience a rather flat one for visitors who aren't comfortable enough to ask questions on their own. You can elect to take a guided tour of the village (adults $20, children 6–12 $12, 5 and under free), which are offered daily on the hour between 10 A.M. and 4 P.M. But be sure to ask about these tours at the ticket booth, as no one is likely to volunteer information on them.

The village has a small gift shop at the exit where you can purchase crafts made by village interpreters.

SHOPPING

Cherokee is in many ways a nostalgic place. Apart from the casino and the ever-growing sprawl of new chain hotels and restaurants, the town adjacent to the Oconaluftee entrance to the Great Smoky Mountains National Park has changed very little. There are gift shops by the dozens here. Most of them, however, carry the same standard fare—T-shirts, shot glasses, Minnetonka moccasins, and jewelry (most of it from the American Southwest, not from local craftspeople). You can purchase some locally made pottery and basketry in many of these shops, but places focusing on locally made native crafts are few and far between. Be prepared, however, when you do find locally made crafts. Years ago you could purchase Cherokee baskets and pottery for very low prices, but today crafters know their worth, and even small items can be on the pricey side.

◖ Qualla Arts and Crafts Mutual

The Qualla Arts and Crafts Mutual (645 Tsali Blvd., 828/497-3103, www.cherokee-nc.com, June–Aug. daily 8 A.M.–7 P.M., Sept.–Oct. daily 8 A.M.–6 P.M., Nov.–May daily 8 A.M.–4:30 P.M.) is located across the street from the Museum of the Cherokee Indian and is a must-see even if you don't plan to buy any local crafts. The shop has a large gallery showcasing both historic and current Cherokee crafts. Many of the works on display have been created by local, living artists whose biographies are recounted alongside their artistry in clay, basketry, and wood. Take the time to admire, in particular, the intricacy of the patterns and perfect handiwork of the river-cane mats and baskets on display as well as the double river-cane baskets made extra sturdy for carrying heavy loads and sometimes even water.

The Qualla Arts and Crafts Mutual also has three rooms devoted to displays of crafts for sale, all of them locally made by native Cherokee. The shop represents the work of over 350 tribal members. Here you can purchase river cane, white oak, and honeysuckle baskets of all sizes, a wide array of the beautiful and simple Cherokee pottery from wedding vases to effigy bowls, smooth wood carvings, cedar bead necklaces, handmade dolls, beautiful beadwork belts and sashes, and finely woven textiles.

Other Shops

The **Native American Craft Shop** (1847 Tsali Blvd., 828/497-6790, www.greatsmokiesart. com, daily 9:30 A.M.–6 P.M.) is on Highway 441 on the left as you approach the national park entrance. The Native American Craft Shop carries many locally made Cherokee baskets of pine needle, river cane, and white oak, as well as Cherokee-made pottery. In addition, the store carries Native American crafts from all over the United States, including deerskin shirts, hand-carved animals, turquoise jewelry, and books on Native American history and culture. The one problem with this beautiful shop is the poor customer service, and the same goes for their associated shop, the **Great Smokies Fine Arts Gallery** (6 Acquoni Rd., 828/497-5444, www. greatsmokiesart.com, daily 10 A.M.–6 P.M.), which carries limited-edition fine-art prints, upscale rustic and unusual home furnishings, Native American artwork and crafts, and also provides custom framing. The gallery is located in the Great Smokies Center across the road from the Best Western.

Bearmeat's Indian Den (4210 Wolfetown Rd., 828/497-4052, www.bearmeats-indian-den.com, daily 9 A.M.–6 P.M.) is an Indian-owned and -operated store featuring a wide array of locally made Cherokee crafts as well as Cherokee healing herbs and herb-based skin-care and health products. The store also has a farmers market carrying hoop cheese, country ham, honey, jams, jellies, peanuts, and pickles. Bearmeat's is located on Highway 19 north in Cherokee.

Though one mile south of downtown Cherokee, **The Old Mill 1886** (3082 U.S. 441 N., 828/497-6536, www.cherokeemill.com, Mon.–Sat. 10 A.M.–5 P.M., open Sat. only in winter) is worth a visit and is one of the newest retail establishments in Cherokee. This old-time country store carries antiques, Civil War and Indian artifacts, locally made Cherokee crafts from over 60 artisans, corn meal, cheeses, and preserves. You can still see the mill's authentic grinding equipment, though the mill is no longer operational.

ENTERTAINMENT AND EVENTS

◖ Harrah's Casino

Added to the Cherokee landscape in 2007, Harrah's Cherokee Casino & Hotel (325 Paint Town Rd., 828/497-7777, www.harrahschero-kee.com, 24 hours) has drawn a fair amount of traffic away from other worthy attractions in the town. Nevertheless, the casino has helped the Eastern Band of the Cherokee prosper, as it helps fund tribal initiatives like the building of new schools and community buildings and services. The Eastern Band owns the casino; Harrah's only manages it.

The casino features over 80,000 square feet of round-the-clock gaming space with some 3,300 games. Those include a wide array of slot machines, video poker, live digital blackjack, and baccarito. Even if you're not into gaming, Harrah's is the best spot in town for entertainment. The 1,500-seat pavilion draws big names in music and comedy with headliners like Willie Nelson, Martina McBride, Kenny Rogers, Big & Rich, and Tom Jones. Check the website for upcoming shows, and call 866/370-3705 to order tickets.

The casino also has its own hotel, five restaurants, and retail shops with many package deals available that combine gaming with an overnight stay.

◖ *Unto These Hills*

The popular outdoor drama *Unto These Hills* (Drama Rd., 866/554-4557, June–Aug. Mon.–Sat. 7 P.M., adults $18–22, children 6–12 $8–10, 5 and under free) has been a Cherokee tourist attraction since 1950 when the Mountainside Theater first opened. The evening drama recounts the history of the Cherokee from first contact with Europeans through the romanticized story of Tsali, the legendary Cherokee hero who hid from the authorities during the removal to the Indian Territory and died fighting to remain in his homeland.

The actors in this beloved outdoor drama are not actors at all but descendants of the Cherokee who held onto their North Carolina homeland. While you're waiting for the show to begin, take note of the Cherokee Eternal Flame, which burns continuously just off-stage. The flame was lit from coals brought from a similar eternal flame maintained on the Cherokee Reservation in Oklahoma to which the original caretaker of the "sacred fire" was banished along with most of the rest of the Cherokee people on the Trail of Tears in 1838 and 1839.

You can order tickets by phone, on the website, or pick them up at the main box office at the intersection of Drama Road and Tsali Boulevard. The ticket office is open Monday–Saturday 9 A.M.–4 P.M. You can also purchase tickets at the Mountainside Theater from 4 P.M. until showtime.

Festivals

The town of Cherokee holds more than a dozen festivals throughout the year, most of them occurring at the Cherokee Indian Fair Grounds adjacent to the Museum of the Cherokee Indian. One that is a true local event is the **Ramp It Up Festival,** which is held each year in March to coincide with the opening of trout season. Those who attend will feast on both mountain trout and local ramps, enjoy local music and craft vendors, and watch horseshoe tournaments.

In May and October, the town hosts **"Cruise the Smokies" Spring Cherokee Rod Run,** a gathering of vintage vehicles from Model Ts to Stingrays. In July, the **Festival of Native Peoples and Cherokee Art Market** fills the fair grounds with Native American vendors from all over the southeast as well as with dancing, storytelling, and singing performances. For more information on Cherokee events, visit www.cherokee-nc.com.

SPORTS AND RECREATION
Hiking
◖ MINGO FALLS

- Distance: 0.2 miles one-way
- Duration: 20 minutes

Mingo Falls

© DEBORAH HUSO

- Elevation gain: Minimal
- Difficulty: Easy
- Trailhead: Just before entering the park from Cherokee on Highway 441, take a right onto Big Cove Road. Go 5.2 miles to Mingo Falls Campground, and turn right. You'll see the sign for the trailhead upon entering the campground.

If you want to see one of the Great Smoky Mountains' beautiful waterfalls without the effort of a strenuous hike, the trail to Mingo Falls is perfect. It's also one of the few easy trails in the Smokies that isn't mobbed with visitors and is a great stroll for young children as well. The hardest part of the trail is the 170 steps you have to climb at the outset, but after that the trail slopes gently upward alongside a tumbling stream.

The trail is prettiest in June and July when the mountain laurel and then the rhododendron are in bloom. The trail is rocky but short, and after curling around a large rock ledge on the left, the falls will rise immediately in front of you. Step up onto the bridge in front of the falls, which roll along alternately wispy and rushing vertical paths for a breathtaking drop of 120 feet into Cove Creek.

Fishing

The Cherokee Indian Reservation provides some often-overlooked opportunities for trout fishing. The reservation has over 30 miles of trout streams as well as three trout ponds, and waters throughout the Qualla Boundary are restocked with brook, rainbow, and brown trout twice weekly. The trout are raised at the **Cherokee Tribal Hatchery** (Big Cove Rd., 828/497-5520, Mon.–Fri. 8 A.M.–4 P.M.), which welcomes visitors.

The open season for Enterprise Waters (tribally stocked trout streams) is from the last Saturday in March until the last day in February. Those public fishing areas include Raven Fork from its confluence with Straight Fork downstream to the Oconaluftee River and then down the Oconaluftee to the reservation boundary at Birdtown. Bunches Creek and the fish ponds in Big Cove as well as Soco Creek on U.S. 19 are also open to public fishing. All other waters are not open to public fishing and can only be fished by members of the Eastern Band of Cherokee Indians.

A good place for family fishing is the **Oconaluftee Islands Park,** which is right in the center of town adjacent to Highway 441. A popular destination for picnicking, swimming, and fishing, the park is always loaded with activity. Situated on a small island in the middle of the Oconaluftee River, it's a good place to bring the kids, though perhaps not the best spot for peace and quiet. The park has public restroom facilities.

If you want to fish on the Cherokee Indian Reservation, you must purchase a tribal fishing permit. A one-day permit costs $7. For more information on where to purchase permits and for a map of fishing areas, contact the **Fish & Game Management Enterprise of the Eastern Band of the Cherokee Nation** (800/438-1601).

Golf

You might be surprised to learn that the Cherokee Indian Reservation has its own 18-hole golf course beneath the peaks of the Smokies, but it does. Opened in 2009, **Sequoyah National** (79 Cahons Rd., 828/497-3000, www.sequoyahnational.com, daily 8:30 A.M.–7:30 P.M., $65–110) is a Robert Trent Jones II–designed course located three miles from Cherokee in nearby Whittier. The course has rental clubs available, a pro shop, a driving range, and golf lessons.

ACCOMMODATIONS

Cherokee is one of those places where you're generally better off going with the chain hotels rather than the mom-and-pop operations, most of which are beginning to show their age. You'll find more modern furnishings and amenities in some of the newer chain hotels. If you're looking for a bed-and-breakfast experience, then check out the options in nearby Dillsboro or Bryson City.

Hotels

Harrah's Cherokee Casino & Hotel (777 Casino Dr., 828/497-7777, www.harrahscherokee.com) is probably the nicest place to stay in town, particularly if you like being close to the action. The hotel has 576 rooms, including 29 luxury suites. Hotel guests can enjoy an on-site fitness center, indoor pool and hot tub, and free parking in the casino's garage. The 15-story hotel is actually quite beautiful, with walls of glass to take in the views of the Smoky Mountains. The lobby with its soaring ceilings and stone fireplace displays a vast collection of contemporary Cherokee art. There are also five restaurants on-site.

Best Western Great Smokies Inn (1636 Acquoni Rd., 828/497-2020, www.greatsmokiesinn.com, $55–119) is located in the midst of downtown Cherokee adjacent to Sacunooke Village on Highway 441 north; it has convenient access to shopping and dining and is close to the Oconaluftee entrance to the Great Smoky Mountains National Park. The hotel has 152 rooms available as well as a restaurant, Myrtle's Table, on-site. Guests can enjoy use of the outdoor pool in season, and continental breakfast is provided free November through March. The hotel also offers a free shuttle to Harrah's Casino.

Fairfield Inn and Suites (568 Painttown Rd., 828/497-0400, www.marriott.com/fairfieldinn, $99–189) has 100 rooms and suites, continental breakfast, and high-speed Internet.

Comfort Suites (1223 Tsali Blvd., 828/497-3500, www.comfortsuites.com, $60–159), with 91 rooms, offers continental breakfast, and an outdoor pool and hot tub.

Hampton Inn (185 Tsalagi Rd., 828/497-3115, www.cherokeehampton.com, $59–139) is located on Highway 19 south and has 67 rooms, all with high-speed Internet access. All guests enjoy a hot breakfast bar and free shuttle to Harrah's Casino. In the same neighborhood on Highway 19 south is the **Holiday Inn** (37 Tsalagi Rd., 828/497-3113, www.hicherokeenc.com), which has 154 rooms available, all with free high-speed Internet access. The hotel also has indoor and outdoor pools, a fitness center, and the Chestnut Tree Restaurant on-site.

Camping

Great Smoky Mountains RV and Camping Resort (17 Old Soco Rd., 828/497-2470, $30) has 251 sites available, including hookups.

Indian Creek Campground (1367 Bunches Creek Rd., 828/497-4361, www.indiancreekcampground.com, tent sites $27–31, cabins $50–135) offers fishing access on the stocked tribal waters of Bunches Creek right from your campsite—if you are lucky enough to have a creekside site. The campground has 68 campsites, most with sewer hookup, though creekside sites do not have sewer hookups. They also have a playground, camp store, laundry, and dump station. Reservations recommended, especially for creekside sites. Cabins are also available.

Yogi in the Smokies (317 Galamore Bridge Rd., 828/497-9151, www.jellystone-cherokee.

com, campsites $27–62, rental cabins $55–169) is a Jellystone Park camping resort with riverside campsites and 31 rustic rental cabins, some of them pet friendly. There are 152 sites, as well as a heated pool, fishing, camp store, and laundry.

Cherokee KOA (92 KOA Campground Rd., 828/497-9711, www.koa.com/where/nc/33173, $33–54) has more than 200 sites, as well as indoor and outdoor pools, hot tubs, and saunas. They offer mini-golf, an outdoor movie screen, fishing, and many more activities.

River Valley Campground (2978 Big Cove Rd., 828/497-3540, www.cherokeesmokies.com/rvcampground, $25–35) has 73 full hookup sites, and 42 tent sites with water and electric; 45 of the sites are seasonal. Guests can tube, swim, and fish in the Raven Fork River, which flows through the campground. River Valley also has a camp store, recreation room, laundry, and cable TV.

FOOD

Myrtle's Table (Hwy. 441 N. and Acquoni Rd., 828/497-2020, www.greatsmokiesinn.com/dining.html, Apr.–Nov., $9–20) is located at the Best Western Smokies Inn on Highway 441 and specializes in country-style cooking.

Brushy Mountain Smokehouse and Creamery (664 Casino Trail, 828/497-7675, www.brushymtnsmokehouse.com, daily 11 A.M.–9 P.M., $3–19) is the kind of place where, if you have room left after the lunch or dinner buffet piled high with smoked meats, endless sides, and a large salad bar, you've got a bigger appetite than most. But this place offers dessert, nevertheless—80 flavors of premium ice cream, to be exact. The ice cream is good, and it should be—it's made right at the restaurant. If you go for dinner, be sure to try the hickory-smoked St. Louis–style ribs. They are only available after 4 P.M.

Granny's Kitchen (1098 Painttown Rd, 828/497-5010, www.grannyskitchencherokee.com, Apr.–Nov. Tues.–Thurs. 11 A.M.–8 P.M., Fri.–Sun. 7 A.M.–8 P.M., $7–11) is a family-owned and -operated restaurant serving up classic southern home cooking served in a buffet style. The buffet menu changes daily, but don't worry—the fried chicken is on there everyday.

Sycamores on the Creek (777 Casino Dr., 828/497-8706, www.harrahscherokee.com, Sun. and Wed.–Thurs. 5–9 P.M., Fri.–Sat. 5–10 P.M., $8–42) is the newest restaurant at Harrah's Casino. They offer an excellent selection of steaks, chops, and seafood. Start with the jumbo shrimp cocktail, and then enjoy several southern tastes brought together in the pecan, pear, and blue cheese salad. Any of the steaks are a good bet for the main course, but the herb-encrusted lamb chops are excellent. If it is Friday or Saturday, place your bets on the prime rib.

Pizza Inn (920 Tsalagi Rd., 828/497-9143, www.pizzainn.com, June–Sept. Sun.–Thurs. 11 A.M.–10 P.M., Fri.–Sat. 11 A.M.–11 P.M., Oct.–May Sun.–Thurs. 11 A.M.–9 P.M., Fri.–Sat. 11 A.M.–10 P.M., $3–20) is a regional chain located in the Riverwalk at Riverbend shopping area. There isn't much in the way of atmosphere here—in fact you may see a dirty floor and experience lackluster service—but the pizza is consistently good, greasy and loaded with cheese just like pizza should be, and they offer a $7 pizza buffet at lunchtime as well as riverside seating both indoors and on the deck.

INFORMATION AND SERVICES
Information

The **Cherokee Welcome Center** (498 Tsali Blvd., 800/438-1601, www.cherokee-nc.com, daily 8:15 A.M.–5 P.M.) is located kitty-corner across the street from the Museum of the Cherokee Indian on Highway 19/441 and has brochures for area attractions, restaurants, and accommodations. Public restrooms are available here, and there is also a stop here for the Cherokee Transit.

Emergency Services

The **Cherokee Indian Hospital** (1 Hospital Rd., 828/497-9163) and the **Cherokee Police** (828/497-4131) provide emergency services.

GETTING THERE AND AROUND
Car

If you're traveling into Cherokee from the east, take I-40 west from Asheville to Exit 27 for the Great Smoky Mountains Expressway (U.S. 74). Continue on U.S. 74 to Exit 74, and take Highway 441 to Cherokee. If you're coming in from the Tennessee side, take I-40 east from Knoxville into North Carolina. Leave the interstate at Exit 27 (Great Smoky Mountains Expressway). Continue on U.S. 74 to Exit 74, and take Highway 441 to Cherokee.

Public Transportation

The **Cherokee-Gatlinburg-Pigeon Forge Shuttle Service** (866/388-6071, www.cherokeetransit.com, May–Sept. daily 8 A.M.–12:30 A.M., Oct. daily partial schedule, $7–14) offers four round-trips daily between Cherokee and the towns of Gatlinburg and Pigeon Forge on the Tennessee side of the Smokies. The route traverses the Newfound Gap Road through the Great Smoky Mountains National Park with a 10-minute stop at Newfound Gap for photos. Pickups and drop-offs occur at three locations: Cherokee Transit Ticket Booth in Cherokee, Gatlinburg Welcome Center in Gatlinburg, and Patriot Park in Pigeon Forge. Local transit service is available at all three pickup and drop-off locations.

Cherokee Transit also offers local service around town, running every half hour from 7 A.M. until 12:30 A.M. daily May through October. There are sheltered transit stops all over town. Fare is $1 each time you board or $2 for a full-day pass.

Bryson City

This quiet Main Street town at the lesser-known Deep Creek entrance to the Great Smoky Mountains National Park is the ideal place for travelers who want to take in the Smokies at a slower pace. There are a handful of lovely bed-and-breakfasts here, a soda fountain on Main Street, an old-time drive-thru on the edge of town (where waitresses still wear roller skates), and access to some of the less-traveled reaches of the national park. Bryson City also holds some claim to fame as the burial place of celebrated southern Appalachian writer and naturalist Horace Kephart, best known as author of *Our Southern Highlanders,* published in 1913, which detailed his experiences living among the people of the Smokies region. The book was somewhat unique for its time in that it did not portray the mountain people in a derogatory way. Later in life he was a tireless campaigner for the establishment of the Great Smoky Mountains National Park.

SIGHTS
Great Smoky Mountains Railroad
The Great Smoky Mountains Railroad (225 Everett St., 800/872-4681, www.gsmr.com, Jan.–Mar. adults $34, children 2–12 $19, Apr.–Sept. and Nov.–Dec. adults $49, children 2–12 $29, Oct. adults $53, children 2–12 $31) offers a variety of traveling options if you're interested in seeing Smoky Mountain scenery by rail. The train departs from Bryson City for gourmet dinner trains and mystery trains through the Smokies as well as for half- or full-day excursions into the Nantahala Gorge. Combination tickets that allow for a train ride and a white-water-rafting trip are also available. A variety of seating options are available, including 1920s coach seating, open-air cars, and club cars with cocktail tables.

Rafting excursion prices include round-trip train fare, lunch, an eight-mile guided white-water-rafting trip, and hot showers. If you're up for the rafting trip, this is a fun way to do it, and you'll likely enjoy the ride if you're a train enthusiast. If you're taking the ride exclusively to enjoy the scenery, however, skip it. Better scenery awaits on road trips in the Great Smoky Mountains National Park and surrounding national forests without having to sit passively on a train for more than four hours.

The railroad also has special holiday trips throughout the year, including Polar Express and Great Pumpkin Patch Express rides. Check the website or call for schedule information and details on special train rides and packages.

While you're waiting to board, consider paying a visit to **Smoky Mountain Trains** (100 Greenlee St., 828/488-5200, www.smokymountaintrains.com, adults $9, children $5), a museum adjacent to the Bryson City Depot with displays of over 7,000 Lionel engines, cars, and model railroad accessories.

SHOPPING
Most of the shopping in Bryson City can be found along Everett Street in the area of the Great Smoky Mountains Railroad station. While there are plenty of shops, there's nothing particularly noteworthy about any of them, as most tend to carry very similar selections of souvenirs and gifts. Among the options are the **Bryson General Store** (115 Everett St., 828/488-8010, Mon.–Thurs. 10 A.M.–6 P.M., Fri.–Sat. 10 A.M.–7 P.M., Sun. noon–5 P.M.), which carries upscale gifts including home decor, Vera Bradley items, clothing, shoes, and handbags.

Watershed Trading Company (281 Everett St., 828/488-6006, www.watershedtrading.com, Mon.–Sat. 10 A.M.–6 P.M., Sun. noon–5 P.M.) specializes in rustic decor and woodsy home accents. **Madison's on Main** (110 Main St., 828/488-3900) carries upscale home accents, jewelry, specialty chocolates, and gourmet gifts.

The Cottage Craftsman (44 Frye St., 828/488-6207, www.thecottagecraftsman.com) is a Bryson City gem. Located in a cute yellow Arts and Crafts cottage near the train depot, it features only the work of local and regional artists, ranging from fine art and baskets to gourmet food.

ENTERTAINMENT AND EVENTS
Singing in the Smokies

Singing in the Smokies (1130 Hyatt Creek Rd., 828/497-2060, www.theinspirations.com, $15–20, children 12 and under free) is the largest gospel singing festival in the United States, and it takes place three times a year at Inspiration Park just off Highway 19 east of Bryson City. The event is hosted by The Inspirations, a Swain County–based southern gospel group that formed in 1964. While the faces have changed over the years this four-part harmony group's sound has not, and the group has been honored as America's Favorite Gospel Group six times; it's not unusual to hear them on national radio airwaves.

Singing in the Smokies festivals are held annually over Independence Day weekend, Labor Day weekend, and on the third weekend in October. You'll not only hear The Inspirations but several other well-known gospel groups, which may include The Sneed Family, Chuck Wagon Gang, and Land of the Sky Boys with Little Ernie Phillips.

SPORTS AND RECREATION
Rafting and Tubing

The **Nantahala Outdoors Center** (13077 Hwy. 19 W., 888/662-2199, www.noc.com) is probably the best-known river outfitter in the region and offers the greatest variety in both river offerings and difficulty levels in the western North Carolina region. The Nantahala Outdoors Center (NOC) is not just headquarters for white-water rafting operations, however. It is something of a village unto itself with three restaurants, a pub, lodging facilities, and even shopping. NOC has several outposts from which it launches river trips, but if you come to the main campus 20 miles outside Bryson City on Highway

74 west, you'll find yourself on the Nantahala River in the midst of the Nantahala River Gorge. This is good white water for family excursions, as it's exciting without being terrifying (Class II to Class III, $37–99). NOC also offers trips on the Chattooga with its Class IV and V rapids ($89–300), plus the Ocoee ($46–91), French Broad ($46–79), Cheoah ($135–149), Nolichucky ($22–109), and Pigeon River ($19–40). NOC also rents kayaks to independent river explorers, provides shuttle service, and offers other trips and courses such as fly fishing ($50–400), kayak fly fishing ($200–400), wilderness medicine ($149–1,950), and adventure photography ($500–550). River rafting is typically available from early spring through fall, though the season varies depending on the river and rainfall.

Rolling Thunder River Company (10160 Hwy. 19 W., 828/488-2030, www.rollingthunderriverco.com, raft with guide $34–37, guide-assisted $28–31, rental non-guided $18–21, single funyak $26–28, double funyak $24–26, high-performance funyak $30–32) also offers guided whitewater rafting trips on the Nantahala.

Tuckasegee River Outfitters (4909 Hwy. 74, 828/586-5050, www.tuckfloat.com, self-guided trips $10–25, guided trips $20–35) rents rafts, kayaks, or tubes for fun family-friendly floats down the gentle Tuckasegee River. Trips take 2–4 hours. Keep an eye out for wildlife: Spotting blue heron, kingfishers, or even bald eagles is not uncommon. There are rapids, but just enough to be fun, not serious white water. A nice touch is the free shuttle that takes you up the river at the start of your adventure, so when you get off the river you're at the outfitters and your car—no bus ride back in wet clothes. Dry off and check out the snack bar and gift shop.

J. J.'s Tubes (1651 Toot Hollow Rd., 828/488-3018, www.bjsdeepcreekrentals.com) is located just outside the Deep Creek entrance to the Great Smoky Mountains National Park, making it the most convenient tube rental option in Bryson City. It's not just lazy floating; there are also some fast sections along this mountain stream, as well as good spots to stop and swim. Rent a tube and ride Deep Creek as many times as you like.

Zip Line

If you're interested in trying out the new sport of zip-lining while in the North Carolina mountains, check out **Nantahala Gorge Canopy Tours** (10345 Hwy. 19 S./74 W., 877/398-6222, www.nantahalagorgecanopytours.com, $69). Located 12 miles west of Bryson City at the Falling Waters Adventure Resort, this zip-line outfitter offers nine zip-line sections on 20 scenic acres. You will probably be going too fast to notice, but the landscape through which you'll be zipping is loaded with mountain laurel, rhododendron, and flame azalea. All equipment is provided, including helmet and full-body harness. You'll also be accompanied by a canopy ranger. Participants must be at least 10 years of age and 70–250 pounds.

ACCOMMODATIONS
Inns and Bed-and-Breakfasts

The ◖ **Folkestone Inn** (101 Folkestone Rd., 888/812-3385, www.folkestone.com, $109–153) is located just minutes from the Deep Creek entrance to the Great Smoky Mountains National Park and is arguably the best lodging available in Bryson City. Nestled in a rolling pasture just beneath the peaks of the Smokies, this farmhouse has offered visitors a quiet escape for more than two decades. There are 12 rooms at the inn, all with different themes and decor. My personal favorite is the Wrens and Warblers room, an upstairs bedroom with private balcony decorated with bird prints, antique decoys, and fluffy flowered bedclothes and pillows. It's a perfect spot for avid bird-watchers, as it overlooks the feeders on the inn's north lawn. Antique claw-foot tubs abound here as well, and the Folkestone has an expansive front porch with porch swing and rocking chairs

providing a front-row seat to the evening chorus of bull frogs and scenes of summer fireflies. Breakfast is included with lodgings, and dinner is available on Friday and Saturday night with advance notice. The inn allows well-behaved and supervised children over 10. There is no smoking allowed indoors.

The **Hemlock Inn** (911 Galbraith Creek Rd., 828/488-2885, www.hemlockinn.com, rooms $144–196, suites $239–299, cabins $144–300) is a rustic country inn on 50 lovely acres on a mountaintop above Bryson City. The inn has 22 simple and comfortable rooms as well as three cabins available for rent. There are no TVs, but there are lots of rocking chairs for taking in the views.

Camping

There isn't much for campgrounds around Bryson City. Your best bet is going to be the National Park Service camping just inside the Deep Creek entrance to the park: **Deep Creek Campground** (800/365-2267, Apr.–Oct., $17) is located just north of Bryson City at the end of Deep Creek Road. Located just inside park boundaries, this campground has 92 sites, some along the scenic creek. Bathhouses are available, but no showers. This campground, despite its seemingly isolated location, is popular with locals, some of whom arrive early to have a better pick of campsites.

Deep Creek Tube Center & Campground (1090 W. Deep Creek Rd., 828/488-6055, www.deepcreekcamping.com, campsites $21–33, cabins $63–169) is located right on Deep Creek a mile from the national park entrance and offers tube rentals ($4 for all day) as well as full hookups and rustic cabins.

FOOD
Restaurants

For typical southern comfort food there are several options in Bryson City, including **The Station Restaurant** (225D Everett St., 828/488-1532, daily 8 A.M.–10 P.M., $4–20), which serves rotisserie-cooked meats and homemade desserts and has full bar. The

Bar-B-Que Wagon (610 Main St., 828/488-9521, Tues.–Sat. 11 A.M.–8 P.M.) offers hickory-smoked pit barbecue made on-site.

Standard Italian fare is available at **Anthony's Italian Restaurant** (103 Depot St., 828/488-8898, Sun.–Thurs. 11 A.M.–9 P.M., Fri.–Sat. 11 A.M.–10 P.M., $2–15). They have hand-tossed pizza, homemade Italian specialties, and subs.

The Filling Station Deli and Sub Shop (145 Everett St., 828/488-1919, www.thefillingstationdeli.com, Mon.–Sat. 10 A.M.–4 P.M., $3–7) lets you fill up with High Test—at least that's what they call the famous Cuban sandwich loaded with Cuban pork, ham, Genoa salami, and Swiss cheese. For lighter but equally pleasing options, ask about the quiche of the day or try the seasonal fruit plate with honey yogurt and homemade banana bread. As evidenced by the menu names, gas station memorabilia abounds. Save room for dessert, because right next door is **Soda Pops** (141 Everett St., 828/488-5379, www.sodapops.us, spring/fall Mon.–Sat. noon–8 P.M., summer daily noon–9 P.M.), which is Bryson City's 1940s- and '50s-themed soda fountain. Stop in to see the extensive collection of Coca-Cola memorabilia and enjoy a treat whipped up with Mayfield premium ice cream.

⟨ Naber's Drive-In (1245 Main St., 828/488-2877) is one of my favorite stops in Bryson City. Apart from the sheer fun of being served by waitresses on roller skates (some of whom look as if they've likely been working here since the place opened), Naber's sundaes can't be beat. They're huge—order one with two spoons if you have company along. The drive-in also fronts the Tuckasegee River and is conveniently located on Highway 19 to Cherokee on the eastern outskirts of town.

Groceries
The **Bryson City IGA** (345 Main St., 828/488-2584, 8 A.M.–9 P.M.) has a good selection of groceries for campers and picnickers and is the only good-sized grocery store in town.

INFORMATION AND SERVICES
Information
The **Swain County Chamber of Commerce** (210 Main St., 828/488-3681, www.greatsmokies.com, Mon.–Fri. 9 A.M.–5 P.M.) has two locations in Bryson City, the main one on Main Street across from the Courthouse, and the satellite office in a caboose on Everett Street kitty-corner from the Great Smoky Mountains Railroad station.

Emergency Services
The **Swain County Hospital** (45 Plateau St., 828/488-2155) offers 24-hour emergency services and is located north of downtown off Richmond Street.

Post Office
The Bryson City post office (130 Slope St., 828/488-3481, Mon.–Fri. 9:30 A.M.–5 P.M., Sat. 10 A.M.–noon) is just north of Highway 19 in downtown.

GETTING THERE
If you're traveling into Bryson City from the east, take I-40 west from Asheville to Exit 27 for the Great Smoky Mountains Expressway (U.S. 74). Continue on U.S. 74 to Bryson City. If you're coming in from the Tennessee side, take I-40 east from Knoxville into North Carolina. Leave the interstate at Exit 27 (Great Smoky Mountains Expressway). Continue on U.S. 74 to Bryson City.

GREAT SMOKY MOUNTAINS NATIONAL PARK

Covering more than half a million acres, the Great Smoky Mountains National Park is the "great park" of the East, drawing some 10 million visitors annually. It is, in fact, the most-visited national park in the country. And while many perceive the Smokies as a "drive-through" destination since the park features only one major highway, this vast wilderness area is actually home to hundreds of miles of quiet back roads (paved and unpaved), some 800 miles of hiking trails, and 16 mountain peaks over 6,000 feet. The park is also home to more than 1,800 black bears, 80 Canadian elk, and some 100,000 living organisms, making it one of the most diverse collections of flora and fauna in the southern Appalachians. Its biological diversity is the major reason the park was named an International Biosphere Reserve and World Heritage Site.

The Smokies, which receive just over $1.50 in federal funding per visitor each year, depend heavily on donations and volunteers to keep the park running smoothly. The park's lack of personnel and inability to monitor visitor usage is sometimes painfully evident. This problem is most obvious at the park's numerous historic structures, which have been extensively vandalized over the years.

From residences and churches to old schools and mills, the park's historic buildings number over 90. Between 1925 and 1944, the states of North Carolina and Tennessee purchased over 6,600 tracts of land to create the Great Smoky Mountains National Park. While some of that land belonged to logging companies, many

HIGHLIGHTS

◖ Newfound Gap Road: This 30-mile scenic highway bisects the Great Smoky Mountains National Park and is the most popular route through the park, with long-distance views and streamside driving (page 32).

◖ Roaring Fork Motor Nature Trail: Offering a one-way loop tour of the old Roaring Fork community, this route takes drivers past Appalachian homesteads and bubbling streams (page 34).

◖ Cades Cove: One of the park's most popular areas, Cades Cove has the largest collection of intact historic Appalachian structures in the national park (page 34).

◖ Clingmans Dome: The highest point in the national park at 6,643 feet, Clingmans Dome has an observation tower offering 360-degree views (page 39).

◖ Alum Cave Bluffs Trail: One of the park's most popular hikes, the Alum Cave Bluffs Trail offers access to an unusual rock formation that makes it one of the most arid places in the east; the trail also provides some of the park's loveliest long-distance views (page 41).

◖ Fontana Dam: The highest dam in the eastern United States, Fontana is 480 feet tall (page 58).

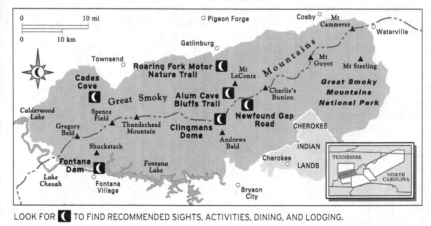

LOOK FOR ◖ TO FIND RECOMMENDED SIGHTS, ACTIVITIES, DINING, AND LODGING.

tracts were the farms, homes, and businesses of hundreds of mountain families. Almost since the park's establishment, the National Park Service has made extensive efforts to preserve some of the historic buildings to interpret the lives of the people who once lived here.

PLANNING YOUR TIME
While most visitors to the Great Smoky Mountains National Park give the park no more than a day's visit, focusing their exploration on an auto tour of the Newfound Gap Road, the only way to do the Smokies justice is

to spend at least three or four days here, more if you can spare the time. The park is a hiker's paradise with some 800 miles of trails, and most of the park's most scenic areas are accessible only if you get out and walk.

You can get a good overview of the park by spending one day in the Cataloochee Valley, home to the park's reintroduced elk as well as several historic Appalachian structures and quiet hiking trails, then another seeing the sights along the Newfound Gap Road, and then spending a third day either exploring the historic structures and trails of Roaring Fork or the more

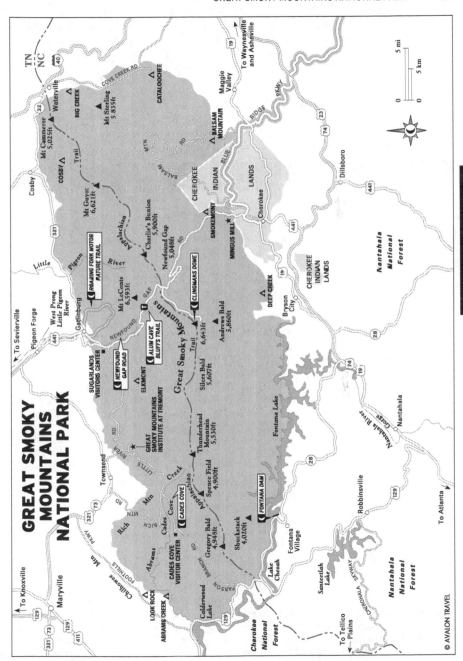

popular Cades Cove. If you have more time and enjoy outdoor adventures, make plans for some day hikes. The park visitors centers have tons of resources on the Smokies' hiking trails.

The Great Smoky Mountains National Park is busiest in mid-summer and October, so if you want to avoid mobs of people (and I do mean mobs) but still wish to enjoy mild weather, consider visiting in spring or

September. You can enjoy more open vistas as well as a lot fewer fellow travelers in the park if you visit in winter—as long as you don't mind the cold. If you do end up visiting the park in the high season and want to get away from the crowds, steer clear of the Newfound Gap Road and Cades Cove and opt for some of the park's many little-explored back roads or hiking trails instead.

Exploring the Park

Established in 1934, the Great Smoky Mountains National Park (865/436-1200, www.nps.gov/grsm, free) was the first of three National Park Service units to be established in the southern Appalachians during the Great Depression. The establishment of the Blue Ridge Parkway followed in 1935, and then in 1936, Shenandoah National Park, the Smokies' sister park in Virginia, was officially designated.

What is unique about these three parks is that, unlike the great parks of the West, all three were carved out of privately held land that was purchased by the states. In the case of the Smokies, most of the land that today makes up the national park was owned by logging companies, and much of the landscape here was heavily logged during the first third of the 20th century. In fact, by 1940, 65 percent of what is now the Great Smoky Mountains National Park had been logged.

The Smokies are something of an eastern rainforest in that they receive more than 80 inches of rainfall annually. This helps account for the park's diverse flora and fauna and its designation as an International Biosphere Reserve.

VISITORS CENTERS

The Great Smoky Mountains National Park has three visitors centers, one in North Carolina and two in Tennessee. The most easily accessible are the Oconaluftee Visitor Center on the Newfound Gap Road just inside the park at the Cherokee, North Carolina, entrance and the Sugarlands Visitor Center just inside the park

on the Newfound Gap Road at the Gatlinburg, Tennessee, entrance. To make the most of your visit, especially if this is your first time in the park, pick up a Smokies Starter Kit for $5 at any of the visitors centers. The kit will provide you a road and trail map for the park as well as information on top day hikes and auto tour booklets for some of the park's most popular scenic drives.

Oconaluftee Visitor Center

The Oconaluftee Visitor Center (1194 Newfound Gap Rd., 865/436-1200, Nov.–Apr. daily 8:30 A.M.–4:30 P.M., May daily 8:30 A.M.–5 P.M., June–Aug. daily 8 A.M.–6 P.M., Sept.–Oct. daily 8:30 A.M.–6 P.M.) is the best place to begin your tour of the Great Smoky Mountains National Park if you're starting from the North Carolina side. The visitors center, which is two miles north of Cherokee on U.S. 441, has a small exhibit area detailing some of the early history of the park, an information desk, and a small bookstore. The current visitors center will soon be replaced by a new structure scheduled to open in 2011.

Sugarlands Visitor Center and Park Headquarters

The busiest information center in the park, the Sugarlands Visitor Center (1420 Little River Rd., 865/436-1200, Dec.–Feb. daily 8 A.M.–4 P.M., Mar. and Nov. daily 8 A.M.–5 P.M., Apr.–May and Sept.–Oct. daily 8 A.M.–6 P.M., June–Aug. daily 8 A.M.–7 P.M.)

is located off the Newfound Gap Road just inside the Tennessee entrance two miles south of Gatlinburg. The visitors center has a natural-history museum that provides an overview of the park's flora, fauna, and geology. There is also an introductory surround-sound film running here throughout the day as well as a large bookstore carrying volumes on just about anything you'd want to know about the Smokies.

Cades Cove Visitor Center

Located about halfway around the popular Cades Cove Loop Road on the western end of the park, the Cades Cove Visitor Center (Cades Cove Loop Rd., 865/436-1200, Dec.–Jan. daily 9 A.M.–4:30 P.M., Feb. and Nov. daily 9 A.M.–5 P.M., Mar. and Sept.–Oct. daily 9 A.M.–6 P.M., Apr.–Aug. daily 9 A.M.–7 P.M.) is 12 miles southwest of Townsend. The visitors center has all the brochures and maps you'll need to explore the park as well as a large bookstore.

PROGRAMS
Park Ranger Programs

Park ranger programs are held regularly at various locations throughout the park and include guided walking tours of historic areas like the Mountain Farm Museum along the Oconaluftee River or hands-on demonstrations at park visitors centers about the wild creatures that call the Smokies' home. Ranger programs also include guided nature and native plant walks and early-morning hayrides around Cades Cove.

The Cades Cove Visitor Center, in particular, offers some fun programs in peak season, including blacksmithing demonstrations, musical entertainment, and basket-making demonstrations. Night hikes are available as well, some of them to the top of Clingmans Dome. Campground amphitheaters regularly host ranger talks and musical entertainment.

For a complete and updated list of ranger programs available in the park, including dates and times, pick up a copy of the Smokies Guide at any park visitors center.

Programs are seasonal, starting in the spring and continuing through summer and fall.

Junior Ranger Program

If you have kids in tow, be sure to stop by one of the national park visitors centers and inquire about the Junior Ranger Program. Most of the visitors centers have Junior Ranger booklets for sale ($2.50 each) with various offerings dependent on your child's grade level. The books offer various activities for children to help them learn about leaf identification, park history, and how to look for particular flora and fauna while traveling around the park. Kids who complete their Junior Ranger booklets are formally inducted as Junior Rangers by a park staff member and get a Junior Ranger badge free of charge.

The park also offers ranger programs geared specifically to kids, many of them hands-on learning experiences. Among the offerings are a blacksmithing workshop at the Mountain Farm Museum adjacent to the Oconaluftee Visitor Center where kids will get a chance to make their own dinner bell, as well as wading programs where kids can get their feet wet in park streams while looking for salamanders and water insects.

The *Smokies Guide,* available for free at all park visitors centers, has a schedule of all Junior Ranger programs available.

Smoky Mountain Field School

The Smoky Mountain Field School (865/974-0150, www.outreach.utk.edu/Smoky, Mar.–Oct., $9–155) offers a more in-depth way to explore the richness of the Smokies and obtain a greater understanding and appreciation of the mountains' flora and fauna, landscape, and beauty. Partnering with the University of Tennessee, the Great Smoky Mountains National Park offers one- and two-day programs from spring through fall in a variety of subjects, including the edible and traditional plants of the Smokies, insects of the Smokies, stream life, wildflower identification, orienteering, search and rescue, and backpacking. The programs take place at various locations throughout the park and require advance reservations; check website for availability and to register. Programs are primarily for adult learners, but several family programs are offered that are appropriate for children 6–12.

ENTRANCE STATIONS

The Great Smoky Mountains National Park is unusual among the nation's parks in that it charges no entrance fee. Friends of the Smokies have donation boxes at Cades Cove, Newfound Gap, Cataloochee, Clingmans Dome, Deep Creek, and Roaring Fork Motor Nature Trail as well as at the three in-park visitors centers. The money they collect supports various park programs and services. Past projects include over a million dollars in support of ongoing efforts to combat the hemlock woolly adelgid, donation of hybrid vehicles to the park, purchase of a search-and-rescue vehicle for the park, and various other conservation and preservation efforts.

The park has 17 points at which you can enter the park by automobile, though the vast majority of those entrances are via gravel roads. If you're up for an adventure, aren't on a schedule, want to enjoy driving the park without experiencing traffic and crowds, and want to see some of the backcountry without hiking, consider some of these less-traveled, if slower, routes.

DRIVING TOURS

For better or worse, the vast majority of visitors to the Great Smoky Mountains National Park barely get out of their cars except to take pictures at overlooks. You can increase your enjoyment of the park's many driving tours by taking some time to explore the history behind what you're seeing and to experience some hikes along the way, too. Even if you're not physically able to do much hiking, consider enjoying one of the park's many **Quiet Walkways,** designated pathways through the woods at various stops along the park's roads that range from a few hundred feet to several miles. Most of them are level, easy walks that let you get close to nature without a lot of physical effort. Watch for the Quiet Walkways signs as you drive around the park.

◖ Newfound Gap Road

The Newfound Gap Road is the most popular route for visitors to take through the park. It extends 30 miles from Cherokee to Gatlinburg and takes about half a day to drive if you take the time to visit some of the sites along the way.

Your first stop along the Newfound Gap Road, also known as Highway 441, will be the Oconaluftee Visitor Center, where you can pick up park maps and guidebooks. Adjacent to the visitors center is the Mountain Farm Museum, where you can explore several original historic structures representing farm life in the Smokies at the turn of the 20th century. You can also access the level and scenic 1.6-mile Oconaluftee River Trail from here, which goes all the way into the town of Cherokee and makes for a leisurely and easy stroll.

Mingus Mill is the next stop along the Newfound Gap Road. It was one of the first historic structures to be restored in the park, and it became an attraction here in 1937, after CCC workers completed its restoration. It is one of 80 such historic structures in the park.

As you travel the first several miles of the Newfound Gap Road, notice that the Oconaluftee River parallels the road to your right. Occasional pull-offs will give you the opportunity to take pictures of this scenic river that was sacred to the Cherokee Indians, many of whom still live on the Cherokee Indian Reservation adjacent to the national park's Oconaluftee entrance. Consider getting out of your car and spending some time enjoying the sounds of rushing water. Notice the variety of flora along the river, including yellow birch trees, the pointed green leaves of the doghobble vine, hemlocks, and lady ferns.

After you've traveled about seven miles, you'll come to the first of several Quiet Walkways along the Newfound Gap Road. Most of these walkways offer short strolls through the woods and the opportunity to get away from the traffic that can often be found on the Newfound Gap Road in summer and fall.

Soon you'll begin to climb, entering a higher elevation landscape with occasional scenic views. If you're wondering about all the gray, dead trees on the mountainsides, these are eastern hemlocks, which are under attack by the invasive hemlock woolly adelgid. The park has some 137,000 acres of hemlocks, most of which will soon be gone forever.

About halfway through your journey on the Newfound Gap Road you'll come to the Oconaluftee Valley Overlook (parking area on the left). Views from this overlook as well as others in the park are not always very clear. The Great Smoky Mountains National Park has, in fact, the worst air quality of any national park in the country, and not all of the haze you'll see is the natural cloud drift for which the park is named. Some of it is the result of air pollution from power plants and automobiles.

At about 16 miles into your journey, a spur road off to the left leads to Clingmans Dome (6,643 ft.), with an observation tower at the summit.

Once you return to the Newfound Gap Road the way you came in on the Clingmans spur road, your next stop will be the overlook at Newfound Gap on your right. At 5,048 feet it is the highest point on the Newfound Gap Road and is probably the most-visited spot in the park.

As you descend on the Newfound Gap Road, you'll find yourself following the course of the West Prong of the Little Pigeon River. There are numerous pull-offs that provide access to the river for photography, fishing, or even wading.

Just before you leave the park, you'll have one last scenic overlook at mile 27: The Campbell Overlook, with views of Mount LeConte (6,593 ft.).

As you end your journey along the Newfound Gap Road, passing through a forest of red maples, white oaks, tulip trees, and dogwoods, remember that this landscape was once cleared for farming, home to the prosperous Sugarlands Valley community. Today the forest has reclaimed the land, demonstrating

HOW TO FIND THE BEST FALL COLOR

Visitors flock to the Great Smoky Mountains National Park for its spectacular autumn color displays, easily making fall the park's busiest season. During peak fall weekends it is not unusual to find traffic jams along the park's main roads. The result, unfortunately, can be a rather unpleasant fall color-viewing experience.

Because most visitors to the park view autumn's colorful stage show from their cars, just getting out and taking a walk can put distance between you and the swarm of visitors. Keep in mind that fall color can be found anytime between mid-September and early November in the Smokies because of the park's varying altitudes. Color begins in the higher elevations in September and gradually descends down the mountainsides. Thus, one doesn't have to visit the park in mid-October to see spectacular shows of autumn leaves.

To find a little peace and color in October, try a walk along the Oconaluftee River Trail with trail access at the Oconaluftee Visitor Center on the Newfound Gap Road just west of Cherokee. A stroll along the Chasteen Creek Falls Trail, accessible from the Smokemont Campground, also offers delightful glimpses of autumn leaves, as do any of the trails veering off from the Deep Creek Campground, which is located on Deep Creek Road 2.5 miles north of Bryson City.

Some of the most spectacular specimens for fall viewing are found in middle to lower elevations, like the sugar maple, which can range in color from rich scarlet to orange and yellow. Tulip poplars also dominate the Smokies, often blanketing whole mountainsides with dazzling yellow leaves. If you stroll along streams or in other damp areas you may see sweet gums, late bloomers in the fall season, that display star-shaped leaves in luscious purple, red, and yellow, often on the same tree.

how quickly nature takes over when man's influence is removed.

(Roaring Fork Motor Nature Trail

The Roaring Fork Motor Nature Trail is one of my favorite drives in the park. To reach it turn onto Historic Nature Trail–Airport Road at traffic light #8 in Gatlinburg, and follow the signs. Just before you enter the national park to start on your loop drive, you'll notice Mynatt Park to your right, a lovely place to picnic right alongside Twin Creeks. This is a safe and fun place for children to fish, and it also has a nice streamside picnic area with restrooms.

Before you actually reach the start of the one-way five-mile loop tour, you'll travel a little ways on Cherokee Orchard Road, which, in the 1920s and '30s, was a commercial orchard covering nearly 800 acres. Once you reach the start of the loop tour, you'll have the opportunity to purchase an auto tour booklet from a roadside exhibit for $1.

The Motor Nature Trail passes through a dense hardwood forest (keep your eyes open for black bear, particularly if you're traveling early in the morning or just before dusk), with the first stop being at Ogle Place, a two-room cabin surrounded by rocky ground and rhododendron thickets. Although you'd never guess from looking at the rustic cabin, this was one of only a handful of homes at the turn of the 20th century that had running water, which the owners pumped into the house from the spring using wooden troughs!

Much of the Motor Nature Trail follows the old roadbed of the Roaring Fork community, which was built by hand in the 1850s and served as the road to the community of White Oak Flats (present-day Gatlinburg). Some 25 families lived along Roaring Fork. As you climb up and through the cove hardwood forest, roll down your windows and take in the sounds of the woods. There are two overlooks along the trail that offer nice views, though they're getting increasingly overgrown each year.

If you enjoy hiking, there are two waterfall hikes accessible from the Roaring Fork Motor

Nature Trail. The first climbs almost three miles to Rainbow Falls and is fairly strenuous. The second is a more moderate hike to Grotto Falls, a waterfall you can actually walk behind.

The real treat along this route, besides the opportunity it provides to simply get away from the crowds and enjoy a leisurely drive, is the access to the old homeplaces. As you descend on the trail and the road begins to parallel the beautiful cascading stream of Roaring Fork, you can visit three more residences, including the homes of Jim Bales, Ephraim Bales, and Alfred Reagan.

Be sure to park and get out and explore these three homesites. You'll be amazed, in particular, at how the Ephraim Bales Cabin seems to be plotted right in the midst of a boulder field. It was something all the residents here contended with, and it made farming a challenge.

As you gradually descend toward town again, be sure to note the Thousand Drips Falls to your left. Though not a spectacular cascade, it's an unusual one with multiple thin streams of water coursing over the face of the rock. Also, make a point of stopping at Ely's Mill at the end of the trail. Built in the 1920s, the mill was not used to grind corn or wheat but rather the waterwheel powered the equipment in a woodworking shop that was once located here. Today, the mill is a shop selling locally made crafts and Appalachian antiques.

Stay on the Roaring Fork Motor Nature Trail as it exits the national park and follow it back to Highway 321 in Gatlinburg. Note that the Roaring Fork Motor Nature Trail is closed during the winter.

(Cades Cove

Cades Cove is the most popular loop auto tour in the Great Smoky Mountains National Park. The route is accessible by taking Little River Road west from the Sugarlands Visitor Center for 25 miles or by entering the park at Townsend on Highway 73 and then taking a right on Little River Road and going 16 miles to the Cades Cove entrance. The loop tour is

11 miles, but you should allow at least two hours for the trip, more if you plan to spend some time exploring the historic structures along the way or taking some hikes that veer off the loop. This auto tour is most popular in the hour or so before sunset, so if you want to avoid the crowds visit early in the morning or even midday (though you're most likely to see wildlife in early morning or evening).

If you take the tour during peak visitation hours, be prepared for slow going and be respectful of others on the loop tour by pulling off onto the shoulder if you want to stop and take pictures or observe wildlife. It's often the drivers who just stop in the middle of the road that make the Cades Cove loop a sometimes-nightmare to drive. If you do get sick of the backup there are two opportunities along the drive where you can take a road off to the left and shorten your loop tour.

Cades Cove is undoubtedly the best place in the park to see wildlife. You can be almost guaranteed sightings of white-tailed deer and wild turkey, no matter the time of day. And black bears are a common sight here as well.

Look for them in the branches of old apple trees, where they and their cubs often laze away the afternoon.

As you drive along, enjoy the scenery. This is one of the most beautiful areas of the park accessible by car, with hazy blue mountains rising up above the valley floor where fields are often a rich gold when viewed in evening light. The Park Service has maintained the rural nature of the cove, keeping mowed and fenced fields so that the community here looks much as it would have at the turn of the 20th century.

Among the numerous tour stops along the way is the Methodist Church, the most photographed structure in the park. Stop your car, climb the steps into the church, and imagine yourself in another time. Many visitors have left little hand-written prayers on scraps of paper at the altar, and weddings are still held here on occasion. Behind the church is a quiet cemetery. As you walk the grounds, notice how many children's graves there are, indicative of an era when infant mortality was high.

About halfway around the loops is the Cades

© FRENCH C. GRIMES

Cades Cove, one of the most beautiful areas of the park accessible by car

© FRENCH C. GRIMES

cantilever barn in Cades Cove

Cove Visitor Center, which has a large gift shop with books on the history of the Smokies, the region's flora and fauna, and outdoor recreation. Also here are the only public restrooms available on the loop tour.

Alongside the visitors center is the Cable Mill Area. This is the busiest section of the loop tour—if people get out of their cars only once in Cades Cove, it will be here. Nevertheless, take some time to explore the historic structures here, including the Cable Mill, where you can buy cornmeal and whole-wheat flour ground on-site. In high season, there will be an interpreter at the mill demonstrating how it works.

The other key feature of the Cable Mill Area is the Gregg-Cable House, built in 1879 by Leason Gregg, who purchased land for his home from John P. Cable.

Around the Gregg-Cable House you will see the usual features of a mountain farm, all of which are original but moved to this site from other places. They include a smokehouse, corn crib, sorghum mill, and a drive-through barn that allowed farmers to pull their wagons inside and pitch hay directly into the loft in short order. You'll also see a cantilever barn; this construction method originated in Europe centuries ago and its deep overhangs allowed farmers to provide shelter to both animals and farm equipment.

As you continue your loop tour around Cades Cove you'll see three more homes, including the Dan Lawson Place, Tipton Place, and Carter Shields Cabin. As you drive this section of the loop tour, keep your eyes on the open fields to the north on the left-hand side of the road. There are many old apple trees here, and it's not uncommon to see a bear and maybe even her cubs taking an afternoon nap in the trees.

After you pass Sparks Lane on your left, you'll continue the loop back to where you started near the entrance to Cades Cove Campground. Consider stopping by the camp store for an ice cream cone before heading on your way.

Cades Cove is closed to vehicle traffic until 10 A.M. on Wednesday and Saturday mornings, when it is available for exclusive use of bicyclists.

Newfound Gap Road

This is the most heavily traveled route through the Smokies, being the main byway between Cherokee and Gatlinburg, and in summer months it's not unusual to experience traffic jams here. Nevertheless, for anyone new to the Smokies the Newfound Gap Road remains the best option for getting a good overview of the park and also provides access to some of its most famous features, including Clingmans Dome, the highest point in the national park.

The route the current Newfound Gap Road follows has provided passage over these mountains in some form or another for centuries, though residents of these mountains didn't realize that Newfound Gap at 5,046 feet was the lowest pass through the mountains until 1872. The name of the gap comes from the discovery by Swiss geographer Arnold Henry Guyot, for whom the park's second-highest peak is named, that the "newfound" gap provided easier passage than the previously used Indian Gap more than a mile west.

A drive along the Newfound Gap Road will take you on a tour that covers some 3,000 feet in elevation, allowing you to experience the varied forest types of the Smokies as well as the differing temperatures wrought by vertical climate.

SIGHTS
Oconaluftee Visitor Center and Mountain Farm Museum

The Oconaluftee Visitor Center and Mountain Farm Museum (865/436-1200, Nov.–Apr. daily 8:30 A.M.–4:30 P.M., May daily 8:30 A.M.–5 P.M., June–Aug. daily 8 A.M.–6 P.M., Sept.–Oct. daily 8:30 A.M.–6 P.M.) will likely be your first stop as you explore the sights along the Newfound Gap Road if you're entering the park from the North Carolina side. At the visitors center you can pick up park maps and guides as well as view exhibits on the people who lived and worked in what is now the Great Smoky Mountains National Park before its establishment in 1934. The park service recently broke ground on a new Oconaluftee Visitor Center, which will open sometime in 2011. The public restrooms in the current visitors center are in the basement, accessible only by going outside and around to the back of the building.

Be sure to spend at least a few minutes exploring the Mountain Farm Museum adjacent to the visitors center via a short walk alongside the Oconaluftee River. You can pick up a walking-tour map for $1 at the visitors center or from a covered box at the start of your walk. The first structure you'll notice on your tour of this outdoor museum is the farmhouse, which was originally constructed by John Davis about 1900. Also on-site here are a meathouse, blacksmith shop, corn crib and gear shed, apple house, and a barn. The barn is the only structure here original to this site alongside the Oconaluftee River; all the other

© FRENCH C. GRIMES

view from Newfound Gap

structures were moved here to create the out-door museum.

During peak tourist seasons, living-history interpreters will likely be present at the farm-house demonstrating early-20th-century cook-ing techniques and talking to visitors about life on an Appalachian farmstead before the estab-lishment here of the national park. You'll also likely see hogs in a pen near the barn. Most farm families kept hogs both because they were easy to raise, often foraging in the forest, and because they typically produced several litters each year. Farmers generally captured hogs in the fall, fat-tening them up in pens before butchering.

As you leave the farm notice the split-rail fence to your left. Split-rail fences were com-mon in the mountains because they were sturdy and could be built without digging holes for posts, an important feature in soil that was rocky. Few farmers fenced livestock; rather fences were used to keep livestock out of gardens and fields.

Mingus Mill

About a half mile west of the Oconaluftee Visitor Center is Mingus Mill (daily 9 A.M.–5 P.M., Mar. 15–Nov.). The mill is operational and open to visitors from spring through fall and is accessible via a short walk from the mill parking area. Built in 1886, Mingus Mill operated for nearly 50 years, grinding corn into meal and wheat into flour for local farmers.

If you step inside the mill, you can watch corn and wheat being ground by large mill-stones. You can even purchase cornmeal or whole-wheat flour ground at Mingus Mill to take home with you as an edible souvenir!

Mingus Mill is not powered by a waterwheel; rather it has always operated under the power of a turbine. The mill race sends water flowing into the turbine, where it pours down inside the turbine tower, generating the power to turn the gears and millstones. Shortly after Mingus Mill was restored in the late 1930s, local miller John Jones operated the mill on a lease from the National Park Service until the early '40s when the mill closed down for a second time.

view from the Webb Overlook on the Newfound Gap Road

The park service reopened the working mill as an attraction in the late 1960s.

Webb Overlook

About 13 miles from the Oconaluftee Visitor Center (17 miles if you're traveling from the Sugarlands Visitor Center), you'll come to the Webb Overlook on your left. The elevation here is about 4,500 feet. From here you'll have your first good view of Clingmans Dome, the park's highest peak, to the northwest.

Deep Creek Valley Overlook

In another mile is the Deep Creek Valley Overlook, which is one of the park's most pop-ular, as it offers long-distance views of pristine wilderness as far as the eye can see. This view looks to the southwest into the roadless wilder-ness of the Deep Creek Valley.

Oconaluftee River Valley Overlook

At the halfway point on the Newfound Gap Road is the Oconaluftee Valley Overlook. The parking area is to the left, but the vast view is across the road looking to the southeast. Here you'll see the deep cut of the valley formed by the Oconaluftee River and the forces of both erosion and plate collision. Before you leave this overlook, consider spreading a blanket and having a picnic under the lovely birch trees whose silver papery trunks line the edge of the parking lot.

Clingmans Dome

As you approach the highest area of the Newfound Gap Road, a spur road off to the left will take you on a seven-mile side trip to Clingmans Dome, the highest peak in the park and also the highest mountain in Tennessee at 6,643 feet. A short but steep half-mile trail will take you from Clingmans parking area to an observation tower at the summit. On a clear day you can enjoy 360-degree views, even seeing as far as Mount Mitchell. However, don't be surprised if you're fogged in, as the peaks of the Smokies seem to spend most of their time in the clouds. But wait a little while if you can: The weather here is ever changing, and a fog can drift away in a matter of minutes.

Newfound Gap

The Newfound Gap overlook is the most visited spot in the park, and if motorists get out of their cars at one place, this will be it. The elevation here is 5,048 feet, the highest point on the Newfound Gap Road.

The first thing you'll notice as you enter the overlook parking lot is the Rockefeller Memorial to your left. This simple stone terrace commemorates the $5 million donation the Rockefeller Foundation made to help the states of Tennessee and North Carolina purchase the land to create the Great Smoky Mountains National Park.

President Franklin D. Roosevelt dedicated the national park at Newfound Gap in 1940. The memorial actually straddles the state line between Tennessee and North Carolina, and the Appalachian Trail passes through here as well.

Take some time to enjoy the view from Newfound Gap. You'll likely see the Smokies'

signature haze settling in the folds of the mountains. Notice the stone walls that line the overlook, most of them built by Civilian Conservation Corps workers in the 1930s. More than 4,300 CCC boys worked in the park during the Great Depression.

You might notice it's a bit cooler here than at the park entrances—in fact, you can expect temperatures at Newfound Gap to be at least 10 to 15 degrees cooler than in Cherokee or Gatlinburg.

Morton Overlook

Situated at an elevation of 4,837 feet, the Morton Overlook affords an incredible view of the V-shaped valley of the West Fork of the Little Pigeon River. You can probably also see the Newfound Gap Road twisting away below you on its way to Gatlinburg. Also look for the twin peaks of Chimney Tops to your left. You can hike to the top of Chimney Tops on a steep trail requiring hand-over-hand climbing from the trailhead, which is eight miles from the Sugarlands Visitor Center and accessible from the Newfound Gap Road.

River Pull-Offs

Between the Sugarlands Visitor Center and the trailhead for Alum Cave Bluffs along the Newfound Gap Road are many pull-offs that allow you to pause and take in the sounds and sights of the West Prong of the Little Pigeon River. Even in summer the water is a chilly 55 degrees, allowing it to act as an air-conditioner for the surrounding landscape. If you're visiting the park in early to mid-summer you'll probably be treated to gorgeous displays of Rosebay rhododendron along the river, but even if you're traveling outside of bloom season, enjoy the dark-green foliage of the riverside thickets.

Campbell Overlook

About three miles from the Sugarlands park entrance in Tennessee is the Campbell Overlook, which offers views of Mount LeConte. With an elevation of 6,593 feet, LeConte is the third-highest peak in the Smokies and also the *tallest*

GREAT SMOKY MOUNTAINS

West Prong of the Little Pigeon River along the Newfound Gap Road

mountain east of the Mississippi in that it rises over a mile from its actual base to its summit.

Sugarlands Visitor Center

The Sugarlands Visitor Center (865/436-1200, Dec.–Feb. daily 8 A.M.–4 P.M., Mar. and Nov. daily 8 A.M.–5 P.M., Apr.–May and Sept.–Oct. daily 8 A.M.–6 P.M., June–Aug. daily 8 A.M.–7 P.M.) is the most heavily visited in the park and has a large exhibit area on the park's geology, flora, and fauna. While you're here, consider taking a stroll along the 1.9-mile Gatlinburg Trail, which departs the visitors center near the restrooms. This is one of only two trails in the park where pets are allowed, and it makes for a nice nature stroll, being mostly level, as it wends its way through the woods and along the West Prong of the Little Pigeon River.

HIKING
Clingmans Dome

- Distance: 1 mile round-trip

- Duration: 30–45 minutes

- Elevation gain: 330 feet

- Difficulty: Moderate

- Trailhead: At the Clingmans Dome parking area located seven miles off the Newfound Gap Road via a spur road just east of Newfound Gap (the spur road is closed Dec.–Mar. each year)

The hike to Clingmans Dome is probably the most popular short hike along the Newfound Gap Road. Clingmans is not only the highest peak in the park but also the highest mountain in Tennessee at 6,643 feet. A short but steep half-mile paved trail will take you from Clingmans parking area to an observation tower at the summit. Even though the trail to the summit is paved and wide, it's still strenuous because of the extreme elevation gain in a short distance, so don't think this will be an easy stroll.

As you hike, notice the surrounding landscape of thick undergrowth and stunted and windswept trees. You may be surprised, if you're visiting Clingmans Dome in summer, at the richness of life on the summit. Wildflowers by the thousands line the path, and in late summer you can pick sweet wild raspberries along the trail.

While it's possible to experience incredible long-distance views from Clingmans Dome, don't be surprised if you're fogged in. Because of its high elevation the mountaintop is often blanketed in haze, and you may only be able to see a few feet in front of you.

The observation tower at the summit rises 45 feet above the surrounding landscape, allowing you to rise above the tree line for 360-degree views on a clear day.

At the top of the tower, the National Park Service has signage to help orient you with diagrams of the surrounding mountains. If you're lucky and arrive here on a clear day, you may be able to see the highest peak east of the Mississippi, Mount Mitchell (6,684 ft.), which is just north of Asheville, North Carolina.

You may be alarmed by the tree die-off on the summit of Clingmans Dome. The forest here is mostly spruce-fir, and invasive species and air pollution have both taken their toll on the trees. The invasive balsam woolly adelgid has killed more than 70 percent of the Smokies' Fraser firs, and you can see their silvery skeletons stretching away in all directions. Pollution plays a role, too. The Smokies receive the highest deposits of sulfur and nitrogen in the form of acid rain of any other national park in the United States. Rain on the high summits like Clingmans Dome has five to ten times the acid content of natural precipitation. Much of that acid moisture arrives here in the form of cloud cover, though Clingmans also receives an astounding 82 inches of rainfall each year.

【 Alum Cave Bluffs Trail

- Distance: 11 miles round-trip

- Duration: 7–8 hours

- Elevation gain: 2,560 feet

- Difficulty: Strenuous

- Trailhead: Alum Cave Bluffs Trailhead parking area on the Newfound Gap Road 8.6 miles from the Sugarlands Visitor Center

The Alum Cave Bluffs Trail is one of the most popular in the park, with good reason.

The five-mile hike to the summit of Mount LeConte (6,593 ft.) offers an ever-changing landscape of mountain streams, unusual rock formations, and long-distance views. If you plan to hike this trail come early, as the two parking areas fill up quickly.

The first stretch of the trail makes a moderate climb through mature northern hardwood and hemlock forest, and you'll be amazed by the size of some of the trees here. The path parallels Alum Cave Creek and is lined with an abundance of rhododendron thickets, which are profuse with white and pink blossoms in mid-June and July.

The first mile and a half of the trail offers many lovely views of small cascades tumbling over rocks. As you hike along, look for salamanders—the park has 27 species. Salamanders love the Smokies' temperate rainforest climate. The easiest to spot will be the black-bellied salamander, which often grows longer than six inches.

At about 1.5 miles, you'll come to a feature known as Arch Rock, which is less an arch than a narrow tunnel formed by centuries of freeze and thaw conditions on this mountainside. Several stone steps lead right through Arch Rock, and after this landmark you'll notice the trail begins to climb more steeply and steadily. As the elevation changes, so does the forest around you, which begins to display more spruce and fir trees.

After another half-mile of climbing you'll reach an area known as Inspiration Point, which affords views of steep, jagged, and boxy slopes often enveloped by streaks of fog. The landscape has changed to one of heath balds and is more open with scrubby undergrowth, including mountain laurel and blueberries. You'll also see abundant evidence of landslides on the surrounding slopes.

The halfway point of this trail is at Alum Cave Bluffs. These arching rock formations create a rain shelter that is less a cave than an overhang that allows them to have such an arid climate in their shadow that precipitation never reaches the dry and dusty soil beneath them. Among the unusual minerals that

© DEBORAH HUSO

stream along the Alum Cave Bluffs Trail, one of the park's most popular trails

can be found at Alum Cave Bluffs is oxalate, a rare mineral that occurs only in the world's most arid climates, making this spot quite an anomaly. Even if it's pouring rain, you'll never feel moisture here. So even though the Smokies are one of the wettest places on the East Coast (Mount LeConte receives over 80 inches of precipitation a year), Alum Cave Bluffs is one of the driest.

The vast majority of hikers turn around at Alum Cave Bluffs and head back to their vehicles, but if you have the time and energy, keep going. Your journey will be rewarded. The trek becomes more consistently steep and challenging as you proceed past Alum Cave along narrow rock ledges, often using the assistance of steel cables to pull your way along. But as you hike, you'll enjoy ample long-distance views (if it's not raining!), revealing slopes devastated by hemlock die-off as well as your first opportunity to see the summit of LeConte.

As you hike, pause to notice the rhododendron, doghobble, and lush green ferns along the path to help take your mind off the steady steep climb, which will persist for most of the remaining two miles to the summit. The last steep section of trail will require you to climb

along narrow rock ledges, then you'll emerge into a spruce forest so dense it will seem like dusk even in the middle of the day. Take note of all the colorful mushrooms, richly growing lichen and moss, and small gnarled trees. This is also a good place to look for salamanders and snails.

Soon you'll intersect with the Rainbow Falls Trail, which leads you to the summit of LeConte in short order. Hopefully you've made reservations for an overnight stay at LeConte Lodge, the park's hike-in lodging facility. There is no electricity or running water available at the lodge, but there is hot food and propane-heated cabins, which after your hike will seem like a luxury.

If the weather is clear, you can easily see 60 miles from the summit. The best place for watching sunsets is Cliff Top, which is accessible via a spur trail from the lodge; if you're here for sunrise, hang out at Myrtle Point. Return via the same route.

HORSEBACK RIDING

The **Smokemont Riding Stable** (828/497-2373, www.smokemontridingstable.com, Apr.–Nov. daily 9 A.M.–5 P.M., $8–48) offers guided trail rides of one to 2.5 hours. The 2.5-hour ride

GREAT SMOKY MOUNTAINS

departs at 9 A.M., noon, and 3 P.M. and takes you along Chasteen Creek to the Chasteen Creek waterfall. Wagon rides along the Oconaluftee River to the old Beck farmstead and back are also available. Riders do not have to be experienced, as basic instruction is provided in advance of all trail rides. Reservations for both the horse and wagon rides are preferred. The Smokemont Riding Stable, which is adjacent to the Smokemont Campground, also sells firewood and ice for campers.

On the Tennessee side of the Newfound Gap Road, the **Sugarlands Riding Stables** (865/436-3535, www.sugarlandsridingstables. com, mid-Mar.–May and Sept.–Nov. daily 9 A.M.–4 P.M., June–Aug. daily 9 A.M.–6 P.M., $25–50) also offers guided horseback rides of one, 1.5, or two hours. Loop trails will take you up through mountain terrain and then back down. You'll pass mountain creeks and see small cascades while you keep an eye out for the abundant wildlife.

CAMPING

The **Smokemont Campground** (800/365-2267, $17–20) is located off the Newfound Gap Road 3.2 miles from the Oconaluftee Visitor Center. It's open year-round, and reservations are required mid-May–October. The campground is shady and close to the Oconaluftee River and, like many of the park's campgrounds, exceedingly buggy in the summer months. The campground has restrooms with shower facilities as well as a dump station for RVs. There are 142 sites available. Firewood and ice are available for purchase at the Smokemont Riding Stable.

PICNICKING
Collins Creek Picnic Area

Located 4.9 miles from the Oconaluftee Visitor Center along the Newfound Gap Road, the Collins Creek Picnic Area is nice in that it offers a large picnic shelter for family gatherings but unpleasant in that its low-elevation forested location makes it a prime spot for mosquitoes and gnats in summer. Unless the weather is cool, you might want to plan your picnic lunch for a higher elevation. There are restrooms here, however.

Chimneys Picnic Area

On the Tennessee side of the Smokies, the Chimneys Picnic Area offers a pleasant place to lunch alfresco. Located on the Newfound Gap Road 4.6 miles east of the Sugarlands Visitor Center, the Chimneys Picnic Area has dozens of picnic tables, many of them overlooking the West Prong of the Little Pigeon River in a cove hardwood forest loaded with rhododendron and impressive large boulders. There are charcoal grills available as well as restrooms. Chimneys is easily the most pleasant and picturesque picnicking spot in the park.

Roaring Fork and Greenbrier Cove

Accessible just outside Gatlinburg, these two entrances into the Great Smoky Mountains National Park offer quiet auto tours along rambling streams as well as access to several waterfall hikes, preserved Appalachian cabins, and some escape from the crowds.

The Roaring Fork Motor Nature Trail is paved and one-way and provides a quiet retreat by foot or automobile as well as lots of opportunities for wildlife sightings. If you travel the route in early morning or in the evening, your chances of spotting one of the park's ubiquitous black bears rummaging through forest mast are pretty high, as this section of the park is known for its black bear sightings. The Motor Nature Trail meanders through a deep forest of sun-obstructing hemlocks, delicate tulip trees, chestnut oaks, maples, and glossy-leafed magnolias. The understory is thick with giant rhododendrons that cradle white rippling and sometimes roaring streams. You can spend as little as an hour puttering along this route or

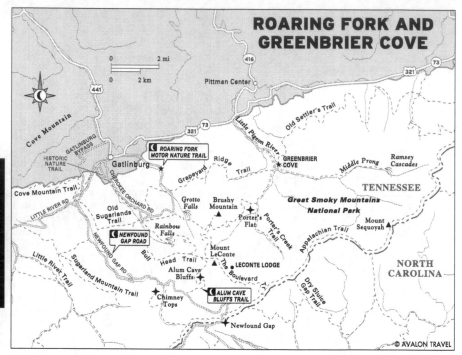

ROARING FORK AND GREENBRIER COVE

as much as a day if you care to explore one or more of the many hiking trails here.

The second half of the one-way Motor Nature Trail actually lies in the original road-bed of the 19th-century Roaring Fork community. Many original Appalachian homes are visible along this route and accessible via a short walk from the road.

ROARING FORK

The Roaring Fork area of the national park is accessible only from Gatlinburg by turning onto Airport Road at traffic light #3. This feeds directly into Cherokee Orchard Road, which hooks up with the Roaring Fork Motor Nature Trail after a couple of miles. Due to its abundant rainfall and temperate climate, the Roaring Fork area is mostly cove hardwood forest dominated by maple, white oak, magnolia, chestnut oak, and tulip tree. You will also notice a substantial hemlock forest here.

Most people come into Roaring Fork to explore the remnants of the small community that once thrived here. Originally settled in the mid-19th century, Roaring Fork supported a few tub mills, a store, a church, and a school. And all of it was located on a dead-end road, now part of the Roaring Fork loop.

Sights
OGLE PLACE

The Noah "Bud" Ogle Place is the first you will see along this trek, while still on Cherokee Orchard Road. An interpretive trail here with self-guiding brochures in a box next to the trail will guide you around this homestead that Bud and Cindy Ogle came to occupy in 1879. Reportedly a local land assessor said the property was not fit for farming, and if you take note of all the rocks around you, you'll easily see why. But the Ogles carved out a living here, even having running water brought

Alfred Reagan Place on Roaring Fork

into the house from a spring via a flume. In addition to subsistence farming, the Ogles also operated a tub mill.

EPHRAIM BALES CABIN

Once you've looped around the upper part of the Roaring Fork Motor Nature Trail, you'll come to the Ephraim Bales Cabin, a small dogtrot cabin built around the turn of the 20th century where Ephraim and Minerva Bales lived with their nine children. Notice again the rocks everywhere: The Bales owned 70 acres here and managed to farm 30 of them. You may find the cabin small and dark as you enter, but that's because windows and doors were viewed only as an opportunity for heat to escape in winter. The larger room here would have served as the main living area, while the smaller was the kitchen. Extra beds would have been placed in the dogtrot.

ALFRED REAGAN PLACE

The colorful Alfred Reagan house was once the home of a relatively prosperous farmer and entrepreneur who owned a mill, blacksmith shop, and store in Roaring Fork. While the exact date of the home's construction is unknown, the original log cabin of the home, which Reagan eventually covered with sawn boards, was likely built in the late 1880s or early 1890s. The house is readily recognizable by its blue and yellow doors, courtesy of early Sears and Roebuck paint. Reagan charged one gallon of corn per bushel to grind corn, a typical fee of the era, and was likely more successful than his neighbors because he worked so hard to diversify his income with many operations. Reagan's Mill is across the road from the house and is all that is left of the Reagan family's outbuildings.

Hiking
RAINBOW FALLS

- Distance: 5.5 miles round-trip

- Duration: 4 hours

- Elevation gain: 1,600 feet

- Difficulty: Strenuous

- Trailhead: Rainbow Falls parking area on the Cherokee Orchard Road outside Gatlinburg. From town, turn onto Airport Road at traffic light #8 and follow signs to Cherokee Orchard.

While the Rainbow Falls Trail climbs all the way to the summit of Mount LeConte, most hikers here take the trail only to the falls and then return, which is no wonder—the hike is steep pretty much without relent and involves a lot of picking your way over rocks and tree roots. That being said, if you're in good shape this can make for a worthwhile hike after a good rain when the falls are spilling over at full throttle.

The first part of the trail passes through what was once an 800-acre orchard loaded with 47 varieties of apple trees and maintained by its owner, M. M. Whittle, for more than two decades under a lease agreement after the park was established.

The higher you hike, the greater becomes the distribution of boulders throughout the woods, making it look something like a cemetery for giants. Take note of LeConte Creek to your right as you ascend. There are many lovely cascades encased in showers of rhododendron thicket. You will also see a lot of large deadfall in these woods, most of them fallen eastern hemlocks brought down by the hemlock woolly adelgid.

You'll know you're getting close to the falls once you start crossing log foot bridges over the creek. The third bridge is just below Rainbow Falls, and if you hike a little further the falls will come into view. Rainbow Falls is not a spectacular gushing cloud of water but rather a thin vertical spire dropping straight down from the top of a cliff. It is actually prettiest in winter, especially if you are fortunate enough to come after a long stretch of cold days that freeze the water into an otherworldly hourglass.

Unless you wish to continue another 3.5 miles to the summit of LeConte, you can turn around at this point and return via the same route.

GROTTO FALLS

- Distance: 3 miles round-trip

- Duration: 2 hours

- Elevation gain: 500 feet

- Difficulty: Moderate

- Trailhead: Grotto Falls parking area on the Roaring Fork Motor Nature Trail

A less-strenuous waterfall hike from the Motor Nature Trail is the Grotto Fails Trail. From the parking area, the trail climbs relatively gently for about 500 feet through a deeply shaded forest of virgin hemlock. Conifer needles cushion the wide path, as it winds through the increasing diversity of maples, ghostly beeches, and silverbells.

You might run into some llamas on this trail, as this is the route used to supply the hike-in LeConte Lodge on the summit of Mount LeConte, and a roped train of llamas makes this trek as many as three times a week loaded down with supplies.

A mile and a half in, 25-foot-high Grotto Falls is a treat for kids of all ages because you can walk right under the falls and mute the world as you stand behind the water's deafening cascade. Don't worry, you won't get too wet, nothing more than a mist will settle over your clothes and hair.

MOUNT LECONTE

The only lodging facility within the national park, **LeConte Lodge** (865/429-5704, www.leconte-lodge.com, Mar.–Nov., adults $116, children $85, includes accommodations, dinner, and breakfast) is almost an attraction in itself. That's because the lodge is accessible only by hike, not by vehicle. It is located at the summit of Mount LeConte (6,593 ft.), the base of which is skirted by the Roaring Fork Motor Nature Trail, and consists of a gathering of rustic cabins with no electricity or running water but ample 60-mile views on a clear day.

Several of the hiking trails that veer off the Roaring Fork Motor Nature Trail provide access to LeConte Lodge, including the Bull

INVASIVE SPECIES ON THE RAMPAGE

It has become an all too common sight in the forests of the Blue Ridge and Smoky Mountains: the tall gray ghosts of hemlocks decimated by the hemlock woolly adelgid (HWA). Like non-native pests before it, including the famous chestnut blight at the turn of the 20th century, HWA threatens to overhaul significant portions of the Appalachian ecosystem. As you drive around Roaring Fork and Greenbrier Cove, in particular, you'll notice its influence on the forest landscape.

A tiny aphid-like insect, generally recognizable only by the woolly white sac in which it coats itself on the underside of hemlock needles, HWA was first discovered on the East Coast in the 1950s. It eventually showed up in Shenandoah National Park in Virginia in 1988, where it has since destroyed 95 percent of the park's hemlocks.

Until recently, foresters have depended on an insecticidal soap known as M-PedeR and soil injections consisting of a pesticide called MeritR to help fight HWA, but neither represents a long-term, practical, or financially feasible option for saving the hemlocks.

A biological solution, however, has been in the works for several years. Several southern universities, including Clemson, Virginia Tech, the University of North Carolina, and the University of Tennessee have been working diligently to raise and distribute predator beetles, another non-native species that feeds exclusively on HWA. The result has been hope for the Great Smoky Mountains National Park, which has 137,000 acres of hemlock forest. The park began working to treat its hemlocks with the help of predator beetles, insecticide injections, and spraying as soon as they saw evidence of the adelgid's presence.

The park's first release of predator beetles occurred in May 2002, but it will be years, most biologists say, for the predator beetles to reproduce on a scale large enough to suppress HWA on their own. Thus far, the Park Service has released 400,000 predator beetles in the park.

While hemlocks may not be an economically valuable tree species, their value to the forest ecosystem is substantial. A common sight along streams, hemlocks regulate ground and water temperatures year-round with their thick canopies. Native brook trout, for example, are quite dependent on hemlocks for shade and cool water. Some species of warblers are known to nest only in hemlocks.

In places where hemlock die-off has been substantial, invasive plants like garlic mustard are coming in to take its place, creating yet another round of problems. The National Park Service has treated over 100,000 hemlocks, through soil or direct injections, along roadsides and in old-growth conservation areas. An additional 400 acres of trees have been treated with insecticidal soap.

For more information about the hemlock woolly adelgid, visit www.saveourhemlocks.org.

Head Trail, Rainbow Falls Trail, and Trillium Gap Trail. Trillium Gap Trail is on the route that the lodge llamas hike three times a week to bring in supplies. The shortest route to the summit is the Alum Cave Bluffs Trail accessible from the Newfound Gap Road, but this is also the route with the most elevation gain in the shortest distance. The Boulevard Trail, which comes in off the Appalachian Trail from Newfound Gap, is generally regarded as the easiest trek to the lodge, but also the longest at eight miles.

LeConte Lodge has a long history. It was built in 1934, before the national park was officially established, and has served as an overnight base for hikers ever since, resting as it does on the fourth-highest mountain east of the Mississippi.

There are no hot showers here, but every cabin comes with a bucket for sponge bathing that you can fill up with hot water from the single hot-water spigot at the lodge kitchen. There are flush toilets available in a separate building. Supper is the same every night. It's hearty hiker's fare—beef tips in brown gravy, mashed potatoes, green beans, spiced apples, cookies, and hot cocoa or coffee—who cares about calories after hiking at least five miles uphill to get here? In the morning, breakfast is equally as ample with pancakes, eggs, Canadian bacon, grits, and biscuits.

If you're accustomed to sleeping in a tent or a trail shelter, LeConte Lodge will be the ultimate in luxury. However, if you prefer hotel rooms with 400-count sheets and cushy mattresses, this place might feel a little bit like hell, with bunk beds in cramped drafty cabins with wire over the windows to help deter the bears. But chances are that after you've made the hike up here you'll just be glad for a dry place to sleep.

If you'd like to stay here, plan well in advance. The lodge easily books up a year in advance, especially for weekends and during fall color season.

GREENBRIER COVE

Greenbrier Cove was one of many communities in what is now the national park. Members of the local Whaley family first moved into the cove in the early 1800s. They were later joined by the Ownby clan, and, at the height of its population, about two dozen families lived here, almost all of them Whaleys or Ownbys. Most families here engaged in subsistence agriculture, occupying small farms of 50 to 100 acres. If you're a Dolly Parton fan, you might find it interesting to know that the songstress's ancestors Benjamin C. Parton and his wife, Margaret, moved to the cove in the 1850s. Their descendants moved out of the cove when the national park came. Dolly is Benjamin Parton's great-great-granddaughter.

Greenbrier Cove is a bit north of the Roaring Fork area, accessible six miles north of Gatlinburg on Route 321 on the right. Greenbrier Cove Road is a dead-end road that follows the boulder-laden course of the Little Pigeon River for six miles. Lined with old-growth virgin red oak, hemlock, and maples, as well as thick leafy rhododendron stands, the road leads to a host of peaceful hiking trails, including the tough eight-

mile round-trip trek to Ramsay Cascades and back.

Horseback Riding
Smoky Mountain Riding Stables (1720 E. Parkway, 865/436-5634, www.smokymountainridingstables.com, mid-Mar.–May and Sept.–Nov. daily 9 A.M.–4 P.M., June–Aug. daily 9 A.M.–6 P.M., $25–50) offers one- and two-hour trail rides into the national park around Greenbrier Cove. Either guided ride takes you up wooded trails along and sometimes through mountain streams. Chances are good you will see deer, turkey, or maybe a black bear. From Gatlinburg traffic light #3 go four miles east on Highway 321 north.

Hiking
PORTER CREEK TRAIL
- Distance: 1 mile one-way to Porter's Flat
- Duration: 1 hour
- Elevation gain: 300 feet
- Difficulty: Easy
- Trailhead: From U.S. 321 take the Greenbrier Cove Road 4.1 miles, park on the traffic loop, and look for gate and signs.

A nice little leg-stretcher, the Porter Creek Trail passes through a wildflower wonderland in spring and past old Appalachian homesites, cemeteries, and an Appalachian cantilever barn, testament to the people who once made these mountains their home.

At about 0.7 mile, you'll see a set of block steps leading up to the old Ownby Cemetery, which dates to the 1900s. Descendants of Greenbrier Cove residents still maintain the cemetery and sometimes replace headstones.

At approximately one mile you will come to Porter's Flat, site of the first settlements of Greenbrier Cove by the Whaley family. The old road that the trail has followed ends here.

If you opt to continue another 0.8 mile, the Porter Creek Trail leads to a waterfall, the soft and bridal veil–like Fern Falls. Return to the parking area via the same route.

Little River Road

Little River Road courses for about 13 miles along the banks of Little River between the park's Sugarlands Visitor Center near Gatlinburg and the park's Townsend entrance at Highway 73. This is often the route park visitors take to Cades Cove, which is located southwest of Townsend. This is a windy stretch of road and the going is slow, almost hypnotic, as you weave back and forth along the curling and scenic stream. But it's definitely worth a drive if you have the time, being the most scenic way to access Cades Cove as well as having a number of worthy sights to check out along the way, including the National Historic District at Elkmont and a number of pleasant hikes.

SIGHTS
Elkmont

The area where the Elkmont Campground is today located along Little River Road was originally begun as a logging town in 1908 by the Little River Lumber Company. The town quickly became a tourist destination, being

especially popular with fishermen. In 1912 the Wonderland Park Hotel was built here, and cottages proliferated. The National Park Service granted cottage owners lifetime leases to their properties once the park was established and then continued to renew the leases in intervals of 20 years until 1992. Originally, the park service planned to tear down the hotel and cottages, but the area now known as the Elkmont Historic District is now listed on the National Register of Historic Places. The park service hopes to restore some of the older buildings, though the Wonderland Park Hotel has since collapsed.

The big attraction at Elkmont these days, however, is the synchronous fireflies that live there. As their name suggests, these fireflies synchronize their flashing patterns, though no one knows why they do it. The fireflies have become so popular here that during their expected peak flashing period each year the National Park Service closes the entrance to the Elkmont Campground to private vehicles (save for registered campers) between 5 P.M.

© FRENCH C. GRIMES

Little River

and midnight. The only vehicles allowed in are the trolleys from Gatlinburg that have been lined up specifically to take visitors in to see the natural light show! Trolleys leave from the Sugarlands Visitor Center. To find out when the next synchronous firefly show will likely be, call 865/436-1200.

Great Smoky Mountains Institute at Tremont

The Great Smoky Mountains Institute at Tremont (9275 Tremont Rd., 865/448-6709, www.gsmit.org) is a residential environmental learning center located along the Little River Road in the Great Smoky Mountains National Park. If you want to have a deeply enriching experience in the Smokies, then this is the way to do it. Tremont is a private nonprofit organization that works hand in hand with the National Park Service to provide workshops, youth and family camps, and programs that use the national park as an outdoor classroom. The institute offers environmental learning opportunities to children from elementary age to adult and also provides training for teachers as well as classroom curricula.

Courses here include multiple-night guided backpacking adventures, guided hikes with naturalists, Elderhostel hikes, geology workshops, photography workshops, bird-watching courses, and even courses in environmental interpretation. Tremont also offers a Southern Appalachian Naturalist Certification program. Camps and workshops run from 1 to 10 days, depending on the subject covered. Multiple-day offerings include meals and lodging at the institute. Tuition ranges from $25 to $950, depending on what courses you select. Advance reservations are required.

The Institute is easily accessible by taking the Townsend entrance into the park on Highway 73 and then turning right onto Little River Road. The Institute will then be on the left.

HIKING
Laurel Falls

- Distance: 2.5 miles round-trip

- Duration: 1.5 hours

- Elevation gain: 400 feet

- Difficulty: Moderate

- Trailhead: Parking area located 3.9 miles west of the Sugarlands Visitor Center on Little River Road

Laurel Falls is easily the most popular waterfall hike in the park, both because it is relatively short and easy, which most of the park's waterfall hikes are not, and because the trail is paved and can accommodate baby strollers. The first part of the trail is the steepest, making a gradual uphill climb through a forest of maples, pines, and mountain laurel, which will likely be in full bloom mid-June to early July.

The trail affords some lovely views into the Little River Valley and has a few resting benches along the trail, so you can sit and enjoy the scene if you like. The trail continues to climb around rock faces. You'll notice the trees are smaller here, as this area of the park was logged in the 1920s.

At 1.3 miles you'll reach the falls, which drop about 75 feet and form a lovely wide cascade. This is a popular spot, and you'll likely find it impossible to get a picture of the falls without people in it, as children and parents alike love to wade here and hop around from one rock to the other in the pool below the falls. You can return via the same route.

CAMPING

Elkmont Campground (800/365-2267, Mar.–Nov., $17–23) has 220 campsites, 55 of them located alongside the Little River. Reservations are required from mid-May through October. There is no dump station available.

Cades Cove

After the Newfound Gap Road, Cades Cove is the most popular section of the park, receiving about two million visitors annually. It is home to the park's largest collection of preserved Appalachian structures, including churches, homes, and barns. Cades Cove is stunningly beautiful and also one of the best places in the park to see black bears, but no matter what time of day you travel this road by car you'll often find bumper-to-bumper traffic. Enjoying the cove by bike is a much better option, and you can do so on Wednesday and Saturday mornings until 10 A.M., when the loop is closed to vehicular traffic.

Native Americans never lived in Cades Cove, though they frequently hunted here, camping

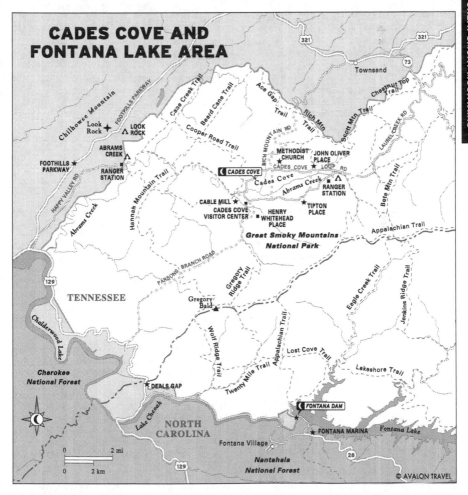

CADES COVE AND FONTANA LAKE AREA

© AVALON TRAVEL

GREAT SMOKY MOUNTAINS

BLACK BEARS:
THE SMOKIES' BIGGEST ATTRACTION

The Great Smoky Mountains National Park is home to about 1,500 black bears, and, not surprisingly, they represent the biggest attraction to park visitors. One of the most common places for seeing black bears in the Smokies is the Cades Cove Loop. Here, in early morning or just before dusk (and occasionally in the middle of the afternoon), black bears can be found lounging in apple trees or turning over rocks looking for insects at road's edge.

But even as the bears represent a delight to visitors, they can also represent a problem, especially when park visitors have little to no experience with wildlife.

Because a lot of bears in the Smokies have become accustomed to seeing people, many have lost their natural fear of humans. And bears that become accustomed to humans, especially humans who provide them with a food source, end up being problem bears. These are the bears that raid campers' food stores, break into vehicles, and approach visitors.

In 2000, two black bears killed a female tourist in the Great Smoky Mountains National Park near the Elkmont Campground. As far as park officials were able to tell, the unfortunate visitor did nothing to provoke the attack; she just panicked and ran. By the time the rangers got to her, it was too late. Neither of the bears had a history of problems, but because they attacked a human both were euthanized. Various Appalachian Trail shelter closures take place pretty much every year due to bear activity.

Black bears rarely attack humans and, unlike grizzlies, almost never attack in defense of food or young. But when black bears do attack, the attack is almost always predatory in nature. This was the case for the woman killed in the Smokies.

Since the early 1990s, black bear populations in the Smokies have been increasing steadily. That's mainly because oak forests in the region have been especially productive over the last couple of decades. Since acorns are a primary food source for black bears, their numbers have increased as well.

Park staff does their best to educate visitors in the hopes of eliminating the opportunity for bear-human conflict. As you tour the park, you may notice placards on picnic tables and in campgrounds, and advisories on the park radio station, advising you not to approach bears and to be wary of how you store food. Right now, backcountry hikers can camp only in designated areas and must store their food suspended between trees, away from the area where they sleep.

Remember to enjoy the park's bears (and other wildlife, too) at a distance. Instead of approaching, use your binoculars or the zoom lens on your camera to enjoy up-close wildlife watching, and employ the following tips:

- Never feed bears. This habituates them to humans and human food sources.

- Always store food in appropriate receptacles when camping, and, if in doubt, ask park rangers for advice.

- Place garbage in bear-proof receptacles if available. Otherwise, don't take garbage outside until you are ready to dispose of it.

- Thoroughly clean outdoor grills in picnic areas and campgrounds after use.

- Remember to report nuisance bear activity to park officials.

In the unlikely event that you should be approached by a black bear, make a lot of noise and wave your arms. Throw sticks or stones at the bear if necessary. This will deter a bear from approaching closer in most instances. But don't run if the bear charges – this will make the bear see you as prey. Besides, bears can run up to 30 miles per hour, so you don't have a chance of outrunning one. Slowly back away, don't turn your back, and make a lot of noise. Often, bears make bluff charges. If a black bear actually makes contact, fight back with anything available to you. The bear may consider you too much trouble and leave you alone.

© FRENCH C. GRIMES

Cable Mill at Cades Cove

in the valley for weeks and even months at a time. White settlers first began filtering into Cades Cove in the 1820s and by 1850 nearly 700 people lived in the cove, most of them farming the wide and lush bottomland settled between the mountains. Among the family names you'll see on the headstones of old cemeteries in the cove are Cable, Oliver, Tipton, Shields, and Sparks.

The new residents found plentiful game here, including white-tailed deer and bear, and took full advantage of the abundance of the earth, so much so that by the time the national park was established there were only some 30 white-tailed deer left in Cades Cove. As you'll notice, however, the deer population has fully recovered.

Everyone who lived in the valley farmed, even if farming was not their sole occupation. Some operated mills, the first of which were small tub mills only suitable for grinding corn. Gristmills were the cove's first industry, followed by blacksmithing, and later, in the 1830s, even an iron forge that employed local Cherokee.

The families here grew orchards and made peach and apple brandy from their harvest. Everyone had vegetable gardens, and most farmers grew large fields of corn and wheat, sometimes rye and barley as well. In addition to eating wild game, most families also raised and butchered their own hogs.

Chestnuts were a not insignificant industry for cove families as well. Before the chestnut blight decimated the Smokies' American chestnut population between 1925 and 1940, families gathered chestnuts by the thousands, carrying bushels of them to Maryville and Knoxville to sell.

When the states of North Carolina and Tennessee began purchasing land for the national park, one of the first large tracts purchased was right here in Cades Cove in 1927. Most families took the money for their land and left the cove willingly. But not all. John Oliver, who was the great-grandson of one of the cove's first settlers, fought the state of Tennessee for six years to hold on to his land, but he eventually lost the battle. Some residents were given lifetime rights to

SURPRISING BEAR FACTS

Unlike their western cousin the grizzly bear, black bears, in general, are not very large. Adult males are typically four to six feet long and weigh in anywhere from 100 to 400 pounds. Females are typically smaller. The Eastern black bear found in the Smokies is usually uniformly black with a square head and round, erect ears.

Though black bears are considered predators, their diets are more than 75 percent vegetative matter, such as nuts, acorns, grasses, berries, and fruits. They also eat insects and carrion and occasionally prey on other animals. They are opportunistic eaters, too, and will feed on human food scraps, garbage, pet food, and birdseed. You will most likely see bears close to wooded areas where they can easily find food and cover.

Black bears may go into hibernation as early as late October. They emerge between mid-March and mid-April. Their most common den sites are not, as legend would have us believe, caves, but hollow trees. Cubs are born in mid- to late January while mothers are denning. Common litter sizes are 1-3 cubs, and cubs stay with their mothers until they are 16-18 months old. It is not uncommon in the Smokies to see mother bears with two or three cubs in tow. Make sure to never get between a bear and her cubs.

Bears can live up to 30 years in unhunted populations, but most live 10-15 years. In unprotected areas, bears' most common causes of mortality are hunting and vehicle collisions. Adult bears have no natural predators and are not very susceptible to parasites or disease.

their homes, and community life went on here to some degree well into the 1940s. The last school closed in 1940, the post office in 1947.

An 11-mile one-way loop tour will take you on a journey around the cove to explore the many remnants of its human history.

SIGHTS
John Oliver Place

The first stop on the loop tour of Cades Cove, the John Oliver Place was the first cabin built in the cove in the 1820s, and interestingly enough, the Oliver family continued to own this property up until the national park was established over 100 years later. Notice the notched corners on the cabin that allow gravity to hold the house together. Residents would have used mud in the chinks to keep out the weather and would have had to replace the chinking periodically as it wore away.

Methodist Church

Built in 1902 at a cost of $115, this church has two front doors, which usually is a sign that the seating was segregated, with men on one side and women on the other, but that was never the case here. Likely the church's builder, J. D. McCampbell, had borrowed the plans from another church of similar design.

Cable Mill Historic Area

Your first stop at the Cable Mill Historic Area will likely be the **Cades Cove Visitor Center** (865/436-1200, Dec.–Jan. daily 9 A.M.–4:30 P.M., Feb. and Nov. daily 9 A.M.–5 P.M., Mar. and Sept.–Oct. daily 9 A.M.–6 P.M., Apr.–Aug. daily 9 A.M.–7 P.M.), which has a large bookstore as well as public restrooms. From here you can begin your tour of the historic area. While all of the structures you see are original, most have been moved here from other locations.

The only structure original to this site is **Cable Mill** (mid-Mar.–Nov., demonstrations mid-June–mid-Aug. daily 9 A.M.–5 P.M.), built around 1870 by John P. Cable; one of Cable's sons operated the mill into the early 20th century. Cable built a gristmill and a sawmill here, both powered by the same wheel. He was also a farmer and maintained a large bell on a pole

© FRENCH C. GRIMES

Methodist Church in Cades Cove

here, which customers could ring to draw Cable in from his fields when they needed mill services.

Also here is the prosperous-looking Gregg-Cable House, which was built in 1879 on Forge Creek Road. Historians believe it was the cove's first frame house built with sawed lumber; the lumber was sawed at Cable Mill. The Leason Gregg family lived in this house for a short time, but in 1887 John's children Rebecca and Dan bought the house. Rebecca operated a boardinghouse here and raised her brother's children after he was diagnosed with mental illness. She owned some 600 acres of land in the valley and lived a long life in this home. She died in 1940 at age 96; the house was then moved to its new location here near the Cable Mill.

There are several typical farm outbuildings in the Cable Mill area as well, including both a cantilever barn and a drive-through barn, a corn crib, sorghum mill, smokehouse, and blacksmith shop.

Tipton Place

On the southern edge of Cades Cove are several more houses, including the Tipton Place, which was built by Col. Hampton Tipton in the 1870s for his daughters, who were known locally as Miss Lucy and Miss Lizzie. The two sisters were both schoolteachers in the cove. The James McCaulley family also lived here a time, and McCaulley had his own blacksmith shop, which still stands near the house. Across the road is the farm's cantilever barn and corn crib.

BIKING

Cades Cove is the best place to bike in the Great Smoky Mountains National Park because, unlike many other roads in the park, the Cades Cove loop is not steep and winding nor, at certain times, occupied with heavy motor vehicle traffic. You can bike the 11-mile loop tour through Cades Cove without the inconvenience of motor traffic on both Wednesday and Saturday mornings until 10 A.M., May through September. During those times the cove is closed to automobiles. Bike rentals are available at the **Cades Cove Store** (865/448-9034, www.explore-cadescove.com, Sun.–Tues. and Thurs.–Fri. daily 9 A.M.–5 P.M., Wed. and Sat. daily 7 A.M.–5 P.M.) for $4–6 per hour. The last rentals are available at 2:30 P.M.

HORSEBACK RIDING

Cades Cove Riding Stables (865/448-9009, www.cadescovestables.com, mid-Mar.–early Jan. 9 A.M.–4:30 P.M., 1-hour guided horseback ride $25, 30-minute guided carriage ride $8, guided hayride $6–8) offers trail rides along a nature trail within the cove for half-hour and one-hour rides. They also offer half-hour horsedrawn carriage rides through Cades Cove daily. Another option is to take a hayride—you'll be pulled by a truck, not a horse, but this is a great way to see Cades Cove since the hayride travels the entire loop road. At various times the park service will have a ranger ride along to provide interpretive

GREAT SMOKY MOUNTAINS

© FRENCH C. GRIMES

Henry Whitehead Place in Cades Cove

history along the entire route. Call for times of carriage and hayrides.

SCENIC DRIVES AND MOTORCYCLE TOURS
Parson Branch Road

If you have a full day to spend touring the southwest corner of the Great Smoky Mountains National Park, consider taking a side trip on the Parson Branch Road. Accessible by taking a right turn just past the Cades Cove Visitor Center parking area, this 10-mile scenic drive will take you on a one-way gravel back road through one of the most isolated areas of the park; you'll come out at Highway 129 just north of Deals Gap on the western boundary of the park. Drive carefully and slowly on this route, and allow yourself at least an hour. The road is full of potholes, and you will ford more than 15 small streams. Don't be worried, however, if you're driving a sedan. The road is not very steep and the fords are shallow.

Shortly after turning onto the Parson Branch Road (which allows two-way traffic for the first

two miles), you'll see the **Henry Whitehead Place** on your left. The story of this house is an interesting one. It was built by Henry Whitehead, a widower with three daughters. He built the home when he remarried to Matilda Shields Gregory, who had been abandoned by her husband and left alone with a small child. Her neighbors came together in the emergency to build her a tiny log cabin, which still stands, connected by a roof overhang to the residence her second husband built her.

Much of the journey follows a small stream, which you will cross and re-cross many times on your drive. Roll down the windows of your vehicle, and take in the sounds of tumbling water and birdsong. As you drive gradually uphill notice the enormous hemlock die-off in the surrounding forest. These trees have all been the victim of the invasive hemlock woolly adelgid. One of the best times of year to take this scenic road tour is from mid-June to mid-July, when the walls of rhododendron along the roadway will be in full bloom.

You'll know you're about halfway to Highway

129 when you crest the top of a mountain and see the trailheads for the Hannah Mountain and Gregory Bald Trails. From here you'll descend. Take note of the many scenic cascades along Parson Branch. You might even want to pause and fish in one of the deep, shady pools here. Once you reach Highway 129, you'll need to take a right If you want to head back toward Townsend or Gatlinburg.

Deals Gap

Highway 129 from Deals Gap to Chilhowee Lake is not technically inside the Great Smoky Mountains National Park, but it hugs the park's southwestern boundary and is a popular route for motorcyclists. That's because this stretch of mountain highway features 318 curves in only 11 miles. You can reach this area, known as the Tail of the Dragon, from Tennessee by taking the Foothills Parkway south from Highway 321 west of Townsend or from North Carolina by taking Highway 129 north from Robbinsville. The area is directly accessible from the national park by taking the Parson Branch Road directly out of Cades Cove, but keep in mind that Parson Branch Road is not paved.

Whether you are in a motorcycle or a car, exercise caution on Highway 129 west of Deals Gap. It's not just the sheer number of curves that boggle the mind here, but the incredible tightness of many of them. There will be many sections of road where it's not safe to go faster than 15 mph. More than a few motorcyclists have been killed and seriously injured on this road. If you're in a car, you'll feel outnumbered by the two-wheeled variety of transportation on this route. The drive is a pretty one, though, with lots of pull-offs where you can let faster traffic pass or from which you can enjoy the views of Chilhowee Lake. There are also pull-offs right on the lake for fishing access, and some have picnic tables.

If you want to prove that you rode the Tail of the Dragon, plenty of photographers set up shop on the overlooks here to take pictures of you on your ride; later you can download photos of yourself from their website for a fee. You can get more information about this famous ride at www.tailofthedragon.com.

Be sure to pick up your Tail of the Dragon T-shirt at the **Deals Gap Motorcycle Resort** (17548 Tapoco Rd., 800/889-5550, www.dealsgap.com, Mar.–Nov. Sun.–Thurs. 8 A.M.–7 P.M., Fri.–Sat. 8 A.M.–8 P.M., hotel rooms $60–80, tent sites $12–16), which has a retail shop carrying Tail of the Dragon merchandise as well as gas and convenience items. There is also a motorcycle hotel and camping resort here, and Dragon's Den Grill and Pub.

CAMPING

Cades Cove Campground (800/365-2267, $17–20) is located adjacent to the popular Cades Cove auto tour at the west end of Little River Road. The campground has 159 sites. On-site is a camp store with bicycle rentals available. They also sell camping supplies, firewood, ice, and park guidebooks. A snack bar has hot dogs and sandwiches for sale as well as soft-serve ice cream cones. There is also a picnic area adjacent to the campground. The campground is open year-round, but reservations are required mid-May through October. There is also a dump station available.

Fontana Lake Area

The community of Fontana wouldn't exist were it not for the dam from which it takes its name. The village was established in 1941 as a town for the workers who built the dam, and, at its height, it supported a population of 6,000 people. Construction on the dam began in 1942, and took only 36 months.

Fontana Dam was built to supply electricity to the ALCOA plant in nearby Marysville for the manufacture of aluminum. In the 1940s there was an urgent need for electricity to supply the industry powering World War II. The electricity produced by Fontana Dam ultimately went to supply power to atomic bomb research operations at Oak Ridge.

The Tennessee Valley Authority (TVA) bought over 1,000 individual tracts of land for Fontana Dam and Lake, resulting in the relocation of some 600 families. Those families' homes, farms, schools, and churches are now all covered by the lake, which flooded five communities. Fontana, like many TVA dams, was thus a mixed blessing. While it resulted in dislocation, it also brought electricity (and jobs) to rural residents in the wake of World War II. The dam also provides much-needed flood control to the region. This area of North Carolina and Tennessee receives more than 50 inches of rainfall a year, and the Little Tennessee River, on which Fontana is located, drains 2,650 square miles, most of it mountainous. Before the dam, devastating floods were an unfortunate part of life in the Little Tennessee River Valley. By anticipating weather conditions, TVA can draw down the dam to accommodate heavy rains. In a typical year, water levels at Fontana vary by as much as 50 feet.

Even today visitors are impressed by the size and scale of Fontana Dam, the highest concrete dam east of the Rocky Mountains. It took more than 2.8 million cubic yards of concrete to build it. It began producing power in January 1945 and continues to produce hydroelectric power today while also providing a popular recreation area at Fontana Lake.

◖ FONTANA DAM

Fontana Dam is the highest dam in the eastern United States at 480 feet and is something of an engineering wonder, particularly given the fact that it was built in the 1940s. It holds back the waters of Fontana Lake, a Tennessee Valley Authority (TVA) reservoir that hugs the Great Smoky Mountains National Park's southern border from Fontana Village almost to Bryson City. The **Fontana Dam Visitor Center** (Fontana Dam Rd., 828/498-2234, www.tva.gov/sites/fontana.htm, May–Nov. daily 9 A.M.–7 P.M., free) has exhibits on the history of the dam, a small gift shop, and a viewing platform overlooking the dam. The visitors center also has showers for hikers and sells backcountry camping permits, which might come as

Fontana Marina

© FRENCH C. GRIMES

a surprise until you realize that the Appalachian Trail crosses right over the dam.

You can also drive over the dam if you would like. The road dead-ends in the national park, but there is a picnic table and grill to the right of the road just on the other side of the damn, providing a lovely place to stop and enjoy the view of Fontana Lake.

FONTANA MARINA

If you have your own boat you can launch it on Fontana Lake at the Fontana Marina (50 Fontana Rd., 828/498-2129, www.fontanavillage.com, Sun.–Thurs. 8 A.M.–4 P.M., Fri.–Sat. 8 A.M.–6 P.M.), which is located on Highway 28 two miles south of Fontana Village. The marina also rents pontoon boats, personal watercraft, kayaks, canoes, and johnboats. Guided boat tours to historic areas across the lake are available. The tours go to the Eagle Creek and Hazel Creek areas, offering the opportunity to see the old copper mines, roads, and other remnants of lost communities that existed before the dam was built. Fontana Lake is 29 miles long with 238 miles of shoreline. Fontana Village resort has a phone service at the marina; Appalachian Trail thru-hikers can call for shuttle service to the resort for overnight lodgings if they want a respite from the trail. Shuttle service is $3.

FONTANA VILLAGE
Resort

Today Fontana Village (Hwy. 28 N., 800/849-2258, www.fontanavillage.com, rooms and suites $79–209, campground $25–35, cabins $89–309) is a rustic resort with 100 lodge rooms and 110 cabins available for rent, many of them the same structures that once served the workers on the Fontana Dam. The lodge also has houseboats available for rent on Fontana Lake and 20 campsites available for either tents or RVs. Guests have access to resort amenities, including an outdoor pool,

lazy river, and day spa, for an additional fee. The resort also has two on-site restaurants: **Wildwood Grill** (828/498-2211, www.fontanavillage.com, Apr.–Oct. Mon.–Thurs. 11:30 A.M.–9 P.M., Fri.–Sat. 11:30 A.M.–10 P.M., Sun. 11:30 A.M.–6 P.M., $5–12) and the **Mountain View Bistro** (828/498-2115, www.fontanavillage.com, daily 7:30 A.M.–2:30 P.M. and 5:30–8 P.M., $13–28). A general store sells groceries, gifts, firewood, and ice, but prices are steep—they definitely take advantage of the fact that there is nowhere else to shop within less than a 30-minute drive. Laundry facilities are also available.

Fontana Village also runs **Hazel Creek Outfitter** (828/498-2211, www.fontanavillage.com, Mar.–Nov. Sun.–Thurs. 8 A.M.–9 P.M., Fri.–Sat. 8 A.M.–10 P.M.). It is located at the general store complex and is a good place to rent mountain bikes or find out more about the guided hikes offered. White-water rafting is also available through a third party. Pickup for the trips is at the general store. **Fontana Riding Stables** (828/498-2211, ext. 6911, Apr. and Sept.–Oct. Fri.–Sun., May–Aug. daily, hours vary) offers trips to explore the Nantahala National Forest as well as lakeside trails. Call ahead for ride departure times, availability, and cost.

Camping

Cable Cove Campground (Hwy. 28, 828/479-6431, www.main.nc.us/graham/hiking/rangerhq.html, Apr. 15–Oct. 31, $10) is a U.S. Forest Service campground with 26 campsites. This is a primitive campground with no water, electric, or shower facilities. From Fontana Village, take NC 28 south 4.7 miles. Then turn left onto Forest Road 520, and you'll see the campground in 1.4 miles.

Tsali Recreation Area Campground (Hwy. 28, 828/479-6431, www.main.nc.us/graham/hiking/rangerhq.html, Apr. 15–Oct. 31, $10) has showers, flush toilets, and 42 campsites.

Deep Creek

The Deep Creek entrance to the park, just south of Cherokee and a few miles north of Bryson City, is more popular with locals than tourists. Area kids enjoy tubing on Deep Creek in the summer, and families find it a great place to picnic and camp away from the park's mobs of visitors. There are also a number of hiking trails here, three of them providing access to waterfalls.

HIKING
Juney Whank Falls

- Distance: 0.6 mile round-trip

- Duration: 30 minutes

- Elevation gain: 120 feet

- Difficulty: Moderate

- Trailhead: Parking area at the end of Deep Creek Road across the creek from the Deep Creek Campground

Juney Whank Falls offers the shortest trek at Deep Creek. Visitors here follow a log bridge to a skinny waterfall surrounded by slick lichen-clad rocks. Along the short and somewhat steep path, enjoy the displays of fern and wildflowers. The falls itself drops about 90 feet total—40 above the log bridge where you'll stand to view it and 50 additional feet below.

Indian Creek Falls

- Distance: 2 miles round-trip

- Duration: 1 hour

- Elevation gain: 150 feet

- Difficulty: Moderate

- Trailhead: Parking area at the end of Deep Creek Road across the creek from the Deep Creek Campground

Just below Juney Whank Falls is a gentler, if longer, hike past wispy Tom Branch Falls to Indian Creek Falls. Following an old road-bed for about a mile, the hike offers a serene forested setting of dark hemlocks and towering rhododendron to a view of one of the park's loveliest falls. You might find the trail a bit muddy, as it's used by horses as well as hikers.

Cascading over rock layers for 60 feet into a deep pool at its base, Indian Creek Falls is so perfectly rendered that its stony terraces appear man-made.

ROAD TO NOWHERE

Just south of the Deep Creek entrance at the end of Lakeview Drive outside Bryson City is a lonely paved highway leading north into the park. Locals refer to the highway as the Road to Nowhere. Decades ago, park officials intended to build a parkway through the Smokies along Fontana Lake. The project was never completed, and the highway stops abruptly about six miles into the park at a man-made stone tunnel. Locals whose families were driven from their homes in this region of the park to make way for Fontana Lake call the road "a broken promise," as government officials had vowed to build a road along the lake's northern edge to provide access to family gravesites.

Cars have never passed through the stone tunnel at the end of Lakeview Drive, but today the visitor on foot can. Beyond the dank and cavernous tunnel is a 26-mile hiking trail that weaves along the northern edge of Fontana Lake. Even car-bound visitors, however, can experience breathtaking views of the Smokies plunging into Fontana Lake from various overlooks along the Road to Nowhere.

CAMPING
Deep Creek Campground (800/365-2267, Apr.–Oct., $17) is located just north of Bryson City at the end of Deep Creek Road. Located

just inside park boundaries, this campground has 92 sites, some along the scenic creek. Bathhouses are available, but no showers. This campground, despite its seemingly isolated location, is popular with locals, some of whom arrive early to have a better pick of campsites.

Cataloochee Valley and Balsam Mountain

For those who want to experience some of the human history of the Smokies without enduring the crowds of Cades Cove, Cataloochee Valley is the place to go. Located northwest of Maggie Valley and just off I-40, this entrance to the park has become more popular in recent years (due to the introduction of elk here about a decade ago), but it's still the most peaceful place to explore the homes, churches, and schools of the Smokies' European American settlers.

One of five historic districts in the national park, Cataloochee was at one time the most populated area in the region that is now the national park. The 1910 census recorded 1,250 people in the valley, which by that time had been inhabited for nearly 100 years by European Americans. White settlers first came into Cataloochee in the 1830s. Most of the valley's residents left by the early 1940s, however, in the wake of the establishment of the Great Smoky Mountains National Park.

Accessing the valley and the elk requires patience. Cove Creek Road is winding and narrow, alternately paved and graveled, and there are no national park signs to direct an unknowing visitor. After zigzagging up and around a mountainous stretch known as the Cataloochee Divide, you'll be transported suddenly into an open valley of endless serenity—miles of rolling grass cradled lightly in the arms of blue-green mountain peaks and watered by pristine and frigid streams. Like its sister Cades Cove, the Cataloochee Valley preserves the remnants of a once-thriving Appalachian community.

To reach the Cataloochee Valley, take Exit 20 off I-40 onto Highway 276. You'll then take an immediate right onto Cove Creek

Road. From here, it's about 12 miles into the valley on a road that is alternately paved and graveled and quite twisty in some places. This road actually follows portions of the old Cataloochee Turnpike, which originally started as an Indian trail. Allow yourself about half an hour.

Just before you descend into Cataloochee Valley, take a few moments to stop at the overlook on your right just after the road turns from gravel to paved after the intersection with Big Creek Road. Climb the short paved trail to the Cataloochee Valley overlook and take in the sweeping vista of the valley below and the mountains stretching out before you

Cataloochee Valley

© FRENCH C. GRIMES

GREAT SMOKY MOUNTAINS

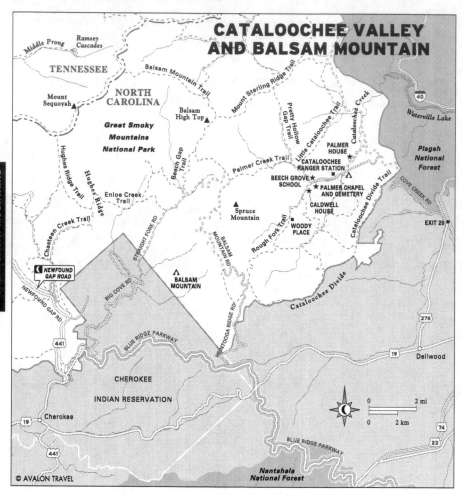

in all directions. Today you will see mostly forested mountainsides, but for the residents of Cataloochee the scene would have been quite different, with cleared land opening up the valley floor and cutting into the bottom of the mountainsides. If you listen carefully, you will hear the distant tumble of Cataloochee Creek below you.

The valley is open to vehicle traffic from 8 A.M. to sunset. Cataloochee is most heavily visited in the evenings before sunset, when tourists come in to see the elk grazing in the open fields. If you prefer to avoid the crowds, come into the valley around midday. You can still see the elk if you get out into the woods and do some hiking, as they normally take shelter in the forest during the daytime.

SIGHTS
Palmer Chapel and Cemetery
The first structure you'll notice as you enter the valley is Palmer Chapel, built in 1898, which now stands empty along Cataloochee Creek, its doors opening to the forest instead of

© FRENCH C. GRIMES

GREAT SMOKY MOUNTAINS

Palmer Chapel in the Cataloochee Valley

to the road. Up the hill behind the church lies a ragged cemetery, where graves marked and unmarked, sunken and new, bear the names of the valley's early settlers—Caldwell, Palmer, Noland, Bennett, and Barnes. The preachers here were circuit riders who typically visited one Sunday a month. Each year the descendants of Cataloochee's original residents gather here at Palmer Chapel for a reunion to share food, attend church services, and care for the cemeteries of their families.

Beech Grove School

The Beech Grove School is the only school building left in the Cataloochee Valley. Built in 1901, the school was open from November through January and sometimes into February and March. Today the school stands empty among overgrown weeds and woods, a leftover desk or two turned askew on dusty floors, blackboards curling away in the humidity.

Caldwell House

Beyond the school is the Caldwell House, a two-story white frame structure with paneled interior walls, attesting to the prosperity of its former master, Hiram Caldwell. Built in 1906, the home has three large bedrooms upstairs. Notice the remnants of insulating newspaper on the walls and ceilings as well as the wood paneled walls.

Palmer House

If you return the way you came and then take a left onto Big Creek Road you'll come to the Palmer House, which was once a log home with a dogtrot connecting its two ends. In the early 1900s, as its owners grew more prosperous, they covered the exterior with weatherboarding. Note as you wander around the interior of the home the remnants of fancy wallpaper on the walls as well as the sturdy rock fireplaces and glass-fronted kitchen cupboards. When Jarvis Palmer inherited this home from his father, he soon began adding onto the home to accommodate boarders. The Palmers owned three miles of trout stream, which they stocked, and charged for fishing. They made further money by renting rooms in the house and in the bunkhouse they built across the road.

THE ELK OF CATALOOCHEE

Elk had not lived in the Smokies since the mid-1800s, but in 2001, 52 elk were released in the Cataloochee Valley, a relatively isolated cove in the northeast corner of the Great Smoky Mountains National Park, as part of an experimental reintroduction of these animals to the area. Since then, the elk population has nearly doubled, and the elk can often be found not just in Cataloochee but also around the Oconaluftee Visitor Center and Smokemont Campground. Interestingly enough, one of the park's elk has been especially adventurous, making extended trips to the Tennessee side of the Smokies and even to Hot Springs, North Carolina.

Adult male elk generally weigh 600 to 700 pounds, while females are a bit smaller, typically weighing around 500 pounds. Males can look especially impressive when their antlers are in full bloom, with some having antlers five feet across. Elk eat mostly grass, bark, leaves, buds, and acorns. Healthy adults do not have any natural predators in the Smokies, though black bears, coyotes, and even bobcats will prey on calves or injured elk. Females generally give birth to one calf a year.

SCENIC DRIVES

Most of the 10 million people who visit the Great Smoky Mountains National Park every year do so via the Newfound Gap Road, so the best way to avoid the crowds is to steer clear of this main thoroughfare into the park. There are a lot of driving alternatives that provide access to beautiful mountain woodlands, high ridges, and boulder-laden streams with virtually no other vehicle traffic—if you have the time and are willing to take some gravel roads and drive slowly. Make use of the Great Smoky Mountains Trail Map, available at any of the park visitors centers for a small fee, as it shows all of the road accesses into the park and will help you get around if you choose to head off the beaten path.

Balsam Mountain Road

The Heintooga Ridge Road/Balsam Mountain Road is only accessible from the Blue Ridge Parkway near Soco Gap at Milepost 458, where a spur road takes off to the northwest. The Heintooga Ridge Road after several miles becomes the Balsam Mountain Road, a stretch of road that is something of a hiking trail for cars. This gravel byway penetrates the park interior just west of the Cataloochee Valley and north of the Cherokee Indian Reservation. It covers about 14 miles of forested mountain ridge.

While you're still on the paved spur road, be sure to stop briefly at the **Mile High Overlook** (elevation 5,250 ft.) on the left side of the road, which offers westward views into the endless sea of blue mountains that makes up the Great Smoky Mountains National Park.

About 3.5 miles after turning off the Blue Ridge Parkway you'll arrive at **Black Camp Gap.** There are a few picnic tables here, and this is also where you officially enter the Great Smoky Mountains National Park. At the **Heintooga Overlook and Picnic Area** you'll have the opportunity to continue your journey on the 14-mile one-way Balsam Mountain Road, a lonely graveled back road that will take you on a nearly private tour of the northeast corner of the national park.

Keep in mind that, since this road is one-way once you're on it, you have to follow it to its end, which will take about an hour and a half if you don't stop to hike along the way. Because the road is graveled and narrow, the pace is slow, but visitors here are few. Even in the summer and fall seasons you're unlikely to come across more than a handful of other travelers on this route. The road is well maintained, too, so you can feel comfortable driving the family sedan on it.

If you enjoy wildflowers, summer is an excellent time to tour the Balsam Mountain Road. The roadside for the first several miles

©FRENCH C. GRIMES

Straight Fork

is loaded with wildflowers, including wild bergamot, tall coneflowers, bright-yellow clumps of oxeye, black-eyed susans, and milkweed that is often peppered with butterflies. Roll down your car windows and enjoy the sounds of the woods, which are made up of spruce, hemlocks (many of them dying), dogwoods, tulip poplars, oaks, cherries, and birch. Watch the play of sunlight on the leaves, and watch for the roadside blackberry brambles that in August are loaded with ripe fruit. If you take this route in mid-June through early July, you'll likely see rhododendron in bloom.

For the first 4.5 miles, the road descends slowly but then begins to climb again. Watch for a small waterfall to your right after about 5.5 miles. At 7.5 miles you'll find access to the **Palmer Creek Trail,** which provides hiking access into the Cataloochee Valley. It's about a 4.5-mile hike to Cataloochee Road from here.

After you've traveled 8.5 miles you'll see the trailhead for the **Balsam Mountain Trail,** and from here the road descends again, more sharply this time. Soon, you'll see rhododendron

crowding around you on all sides. After about 11 miles, you'll notice a small stream cascading down the slopes. Shortly, your route will begin to parallel **Straight Fork,** a scenic boulder-laden stream and one of the tributaries of the Oconaluftee River. At 13 miles the road becomes two-way again, and you'll have many opportunities to pull off and take photos of the cascading waters of Straight Fork, which you will follow out of the park and onto Straight Fork Road, which cuts through the Cherokee Indian Reservation and rejoins Highway 441 at Cherokee.

HIKING
Woody Place

- Distance: 2 miles round-trip

- Duration: 1 hour

- Elevation gain: None

- Difficulty: Easy

- Trailhead: At the dead end of the road just past the Caldwell House in Cataloochee Valley

This wide and level trail to the former home of Jonathan Woody offers a pleasant hike through the forest alongside a pretty stream. It is not uncommon to see elk foraging in the woods near the trail, but remember to keep your distance from these large animals, particularly during rutting season. The hike offers a cool escape on summer days, as it passes through hardwood forest, and the trail is bordered by green ferns and arching rhododendron.

You will cross the stream several times on this hike with the help of log bridges. As you cross, note how the old road on which you are walking fords the stream, providing crossing for horses and wagons.

After you've continued your forest walk for about a mile, the trail will open to a sunny clearing where the two-story white frame Woody house stands. Covered in lap siding and shingled with hand-cut shakes, the home looks much as it would have when the Woody family

GREAT SMOKY MOUNTAINS

© FRENCH C. GRIMES

Woody Place in the Cataloochee Valley

lived here at the turn of the 20th century. Take some time to sit on the front porch and listen to the adjacent stream, and imagine how it must have felt to live here when Cataloochee was a busier and thriving community.

Many of the park's historic structures have been damaged by vandalism, and one thing that distinguishes the Woody house from others you will see in the park (especially those one can visit without a hike) is that there is no graffiti marring the walls. Remember to respect these emblems of life in the Smokies long ago, and leave no trace when you depart. As you wander around the Woody residence, note that this was a prosperous home. Carved mantelpieces remain intact in the home's main rooms, and there are three large bedrooms upstairs.

Adjacent to the residence is an old springhouse. As you walk around be alert for snakes, who seem to enjoy this clearing for sunning themselves in the afternoon. Return to your vehicle via the same trail.

CAMPING

The **Cataloochee Campground** (800/365-2267, Mar.–Oct., $17) is one of the park's more secluded camping options, though you may often find it full on summer weekends. The campground is open year-round and has 27 campsites, some of them on Cataloochee Creek, as well as restrooms (the only ones in the valley apart from portable toilets). There are no hookups here and no bathhouse.

The **Balsam Mountain Campground** (800/365-2267, May–Oct., $14) is a very small and surprisingly popular national park campground accessible off the Heintooga Ridge Road spur off the Blue Ridge Parkway at Milepost 458. With 46 campsites, it's a good place to camp if you're planning on exploring some of the trails accessible off the Balsam Mountain Road. There are restrooms but no showers. This somewhat crowded campground nestled on a narrow ridge also has its own half-mile nature trail.

Practicalities

INFORMATION

Park headquarters is located adjacent to the **Sugarlands Visitor Center** (1420 Little River Rd., 865/436-1200, Dec.–Feb. daily 8 A.M.–4 P.M., Mar. and Nov. daily 8 A.M.–5 P.M., Apr.–May and Sept.–Oct. daily 8 A.M.–6 P.M., June–Aug. daily 8 A.M.–7 P.M.) but is not open to the public. Sugarlands is the park's main visitors center.

EMERGENCY SERVICES

For emergency services in the Great Smoky Mountains National Park, you can always call 911. But you can also contact park headquarters, particularly if the issue is a fire or safety hazard, at 865/436-9171. Emergency services are also available through the Cherokee Police Department at 828/497-4131, or the Gatlinburg Police Department at 865/436-5181.

GETTING THERE

The easiest route if you're coming into the Great Smoky Mountains National Park from the north or west is to take I-40 from Knoxville, Tennessee, to U.S. 66 at Exit 407. U.S. 66 will feed into U.S. 441 south to Gatlinburg. Stay on 441 all the way to the park entrance. While the simplest route, this is also the busiest, and it could take you a full hour or more to reach the park. An alternate option is to take Exit 435 off I-40 and follow U.S. 321 to Gatlinburg.

If you've flown into McGhee-Tyson Airport outside Knoxville, then your best bet is to avoid Knoxville altogether and head south on Highway 129 to Maryville. At Maryville, take U.S. 321 north to the park entrance at Townsend or to Pigeon Forge, where you will take a right onto U.S. 441 and follow it into the national park.

If you're coming in from the south, take U.S. 441 north to Cherokee, North Carolina. U.S. 441 takes you right to the park's Oconaluftee entrance.

From the east, follow I-40 west of Asheville, North Carolina, to U.S. 23/74 (the Great Smoky Mountains Expressway). Stay on the Expressway until you reach the exit for U.S. 441 north, and follow 441 into Cherokee.

There is no public transportation to the park.

GREAT SMOKY MOUNTAINS

TENNESSEE FOOTHILLS

The Tennessee side of the Smokies, home to country music legend Dolly Parton, has often gotten bad marks among more cultured travelers and those more interested in scenery and outdoor recreation than theme parks and dinner theaters. With its outlet malls, bungee jumping, and Ripley's museums, this area has a fair amount to entice a younger set and perhaps very little, on the surface, to draw the independent traveler. But not so fast: One wouldn't want to overlook unique places like the Great Smoky Arts and Crafts Community outside Gatlinburg, which features studio and gallery tours of over 100 local artists and crafters. Even the Dollywood theme park might surprise you—carefully designed to emphasize greenery and scenery, the park is home to the largest gathering of publicly visible, non-releasable

bald eagles in America, a real carriage works, a blacksmith shop, and dozens of venues for first-rate bluegrass and country music. The foothills also offer access to outfitters who can provide white-water rafting, horseback riding, and even back-road Hummer tours through the Smokies.

Prior to the creation of the Great Smoky Mountains National Park and World War II, the advent of which brought jobs and rural electricity to the area with the establishment of the Tennessee Valley Authority, the Tennessee Foothills were a largely impoverished area, and there is still an often startling difference between rich and poor in the region. On the whole, however, tourism and the industry drawn here by the region's countless reservoirs have given East Tennessee a level of

HIGHLIGHTS

◖ Arrowmont School of Arts and Crafts: Arrowmont is a nationally recognized school of traditional arts instruction established in 1945 (page 71).

◖ Great Smoky Arts and Crafts Community: The largest community of independent artisans in the nation, the Great Smoky Arts and Crafts community has more than 100 members (page 73).

◖ Ober Gatlinburg: The largest aerial tramway in the country takes visitors to Gatlinburg's mountaintop ski resort (page 76).

◖ Dollywood: Grounded in the history, culture, and music of the southern Appalachians, Dollywood is the country legend's namesake theme park (page 85).

◖ Old Mill Square: A still-operating gristmill in Pigeon Forge is now the centerpiece of a square of shops devoted to reviving Appalachian arts (page 89).

LOOK FOR ◖ TO FIND RECOMMENDED SIGHTS, ACTIVITIES, DINING, AND LODGING.

economic prosperity that has drawn a strong influx of retirees and vacation homeowners to the region in the last decade. The result is a sometimes bewildering mix of cultural identities that nevertheless makes the region worthy of a visit, whether your preference is amusement and water parks or local crafts and outdoor recreation.

PLANNING YOUR TIME

Depending on your level of interest in sometimes over-the-top attractions, you could spend anywhere from a weekend to more than a week in the Tennessee Foothills and still not do all there is to do. If you're interested in the Appalachian heritage crafts of the Smokies, then you should allow at least half a day if not a full day to explore the Great Smoky Arts and Crafts Community outside Gatlinburg. Allow another day to take in the many attractions of Gatlinburg itself from Ober Gatlinburg to Ripley's Aquarium of the Smokies.

If you are brave enough to withstand the masses in Pigeon Forge, then be sure to visit Old Mill Square, as well as spend a day at Dollywood, which is loaded with great musical shows and has many demonstrating heritage crafters. Allow two or three days if you want to explore the town's numerous and sometimes

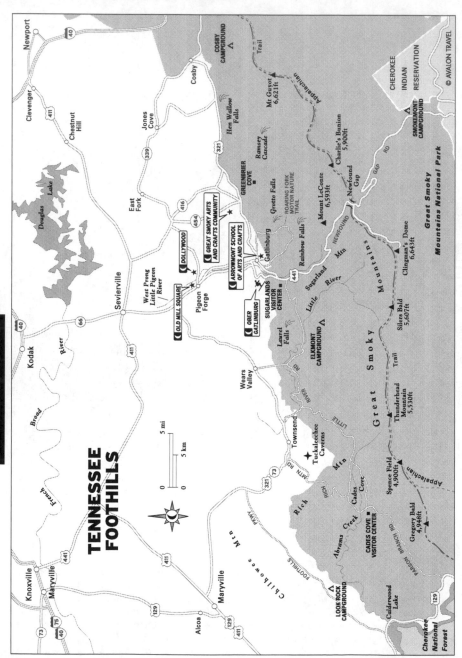

TENNESSEE FOOTHILLS

ridiculous amusements, ranging from Titanic Pigeon Forge to indoor sky diving.

Those seeking a little more peace and serenity on the Tennessee side will probably want to stick to the Townsend area.

There really is no ideal time to visit the Tennessee Foothills—at least the Gatlinburg and Pigeon Forge area—to avoid masses of tourists, as both towns enjoy pretty heavy visitation even in winter when special events keep the local tourism economies bustling through the colder weather. That being said, the busiest time, as with the rest of the Smokies, is undoubtedly mid-summer and fall.

Gatlinburg

Though not as built up as its neighbor Pigeon Forge, Gatlinburg is definitely a tourist town. During busy seasons, the main street through town is almost impassable by car. But past the T-shirt shops and neon-lighted Ripley's museums are some worthwhile places to check out, including the Great Smoky Arts and Crafts Community and the Arrowcraft Gallery. And if you get a little ways outside of town, you can find some peaceful inns as well.

Gatlinburg, though it has the distinction of being called a "city," is only two miles long by five miles wide, its growth likely curbed by the national park on its southern border and the steep mountainsides that border it everywhere else.

What is today known as Gatlinburg was once the community of White Oak Flats, and some local families can trace their roots to that era. How the town's name changed to Gatlinburg is something of a mystery and maybe more legend than truth, but the local story claims that a man named Radford Gatlin opened a general store here in the 1850s, and as part of his agreement to handle the post office operations the community postmark became Gatlinburg.

Gatlinburg is known for many things, not the least of which is its number of wedding chapels. There are 15 of them, and the city has become known as the "wedding capital of the South" over the years. Each year 600,000 people come to Gatlinburg to get married or to witness a wedding, making romance quite an industry here. Only Las Vegas is a more popular place to say "I do."

SIGHTS
◖ Arrowmont School of Arts and Crafts

The Arrowmont School of Arts and Crafts (556 Parkway, 865/436-5860, www.arrowmont.org, June–Oct. Mon.–Sat. 8:30 A.M.–4:30 P.M., workshops $275–1,400) was founded in 1945. Prior to 1945, the campus had been the Pi Beta Phi settlement school, founded in 1912, a philanthropy project of the Pi Beta Phi women's fraternity, which sought to bring basic education and health services to the children of the extremely impoverished area. Early on, the fraternity recognized the unique nature of the crafts that the mountain people produced. This led to the school providing a weaving teacher and later more vocational education. In 1926 the fraternity established the Arrowcraft shop to market the handicrafts of the local people. Today the school has a gallery showcasing exhibits of regional artists and provides weekend and one- and two-week workshops for adults in spring, summer, and fall. If you want to get close to the true and historic culture of the Smokies, signing up for a workshop here is the way to do it. You will come out surprisingly proficient in the craft you choose because instruction is intensive and focused. They offer classes in both contemporary and traditional art in areas such as fiber arts, pottery, metal and jewelry, and many others.

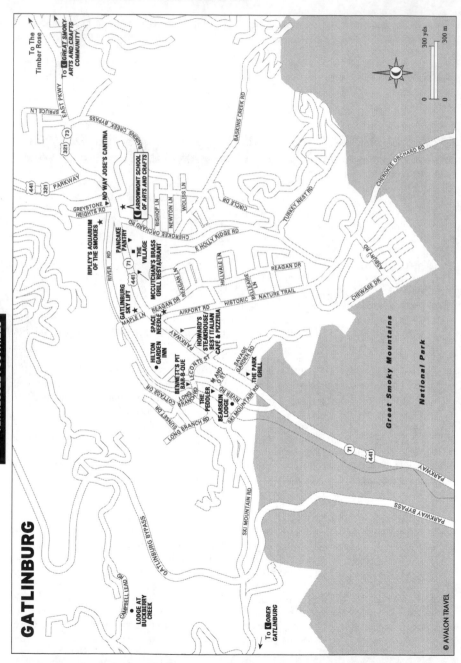

TENNESSEE FOOTHILLS

GATLINBURG

© AVALON TRAVEL

Ripley's Aquarium of the Smokies

There are tons of Ripley's attractions in Gatlinburg as well as in neighboring Pigeon Forge. Unless you have kids in tow, however, you can probably skip them, as they are, for the most part, cheesy at best. One exception is Ripley's Aquarium of the Smokies (88 River Rd., 888/240-1358, http://gatlinburg. ripleyaquariums.com, May–Sept. daily 9 A.M.– 11 P.M., Oct.–Apr. Sun.–Thurs. 9 A.M.–9 P.M., Fri.–Sat. 9 A.M.–11 P.M., adults $19, children 6–11 $10, children 2–5 $4), which is the largest aquarium in Tennessee, holding some 1.4 million gallons of water. My favorite part is the 340-foot-long glidepath that takes you on a journey under the shark lagoon where sand tiger sharks, nurse sharks, and even stingrays glide overheard. The aquarium has dive shows every two hours. Displays here allow you to touch horseshoe crabs and stingrays as well as watch colorful tropical fish swim through a coral reef display.

There are two restaurants in the aquarium as well as a huge gift shop selling a pretty massive collection of marine-themed toys and gifts.

Gatlinburg Sky Lift

The Gatlinburg Sky Lift (865/436-4307, www.gatlinburgskylift.com, Apr.–May daily 9 A.M.–9 P.M., June–Aug. daily 9 A.M.– 11 P.M., Sept.–Oct. daily 9 A.M.–9 P.M., adults $12, children $9) is essentially a ski lift that takes you to the top of a mountain where you can catch a sparkling view of Gatlinburg after dark (which is the best time to go) and also all the darkness beyond, including the sloping shadows of the mountains of the national park. The lift climbs 1,800 feet, dropping you off for a visit to the mountaintop snack bar and gift shop. The lift is located on the Parkway in the center of downtown—you can't miss it.

Space Needle

The Space Needle (115 Historic Nature Trail, 865/436-4629, www.gatlinburgspaceneedle.com, Sun.–Thurs. 10 A.M.–11 P.M., Fri.–Sat. 9 A.M.–midnight, winter hours may vary, adults $7.25, seniors $5, children 5–12 $3, children 4 and under free) is another of Gatlinburg's over-the-top attractions that has its redeeming qualities. If you're looking for a way to kill time after dark, take the elevator to the top of this 407-foot tower at the center of downtown for some glistening views of downtown Gatlinburg at nightfall. If you reach the top of the Space Needle just after sundown, you'll be able to trace the faint outlines of Mount LeConte and Greenbrier Pinnacle to the northeast. Below the space needle is a 25,000-square-foot arcade with video games, laser tag, a virtual reality roller coaster simulator, a gift shop, and restrooms.

SHOPPING

While Gatlinburg is home to some 400 specialty shops, most of those along the Parkway that cuts through the center of town are decidedly touristy. To find locally made items and higher-quality merchandise that might make for a meaningful souvenir for years to come, you have to dig a little deeper.

◖ Great Smoky Arts and Crafts Community

An often overlooked treasure of Gatlinburg's otherwise "touristy" atmosphere is the Great Smoky Arts and Crafts Community (800/565-7330, www.gatlinburgcrafts.com). Established in 1937, it is the largest independent organization of artisans in the United States with more than 100 studios, shops, and galleries located along its eight-mile loop on Glades Road, Buckhorn Road, and Highway 321 about three miles east of downtown Gatlinburg.

What's special about this community is not just the crafts but the fact that visitors can actually interact with the artists, many of whom own and operate their own galleries. Be sure to look for the Great Smoky Arts and Crafts signs, however, which ensure the galleries display the genuine handiwork of local and regional artisans. You can pick up a map of the community at one of Gatlinburg's visitors centers. If you

WEDDING CAPITAL OF THE SOUTH

Even the most cursory drive through Gatlinburg will clue you in to the fact that this is a popular place to get married. Wedding chapels abound in the town and surrounding hills, and some 20,000 couples tie the knot here every year. Las Vegas is the only place in America with more weddings than Gatlinburg. That's why the town has come to be known as the "wedding capital of the South."

A few celebrities have even jumped the broom here, including Billy Ray Cyrus and Patty Loveless. But why?

Part of the reason is that Tennessee requires no blood tests or waiting period before getting married, making it a relatively easy place to get hitched. Plus, there are plenty of things to drive romance here, including the

beautiful scenery and oodles of romantic accommodations. But then comes the question: Which came first, the cabin rentals with heart-shaped whirlpool tubs or the couples seeking nuptials?

We may never know.

But if you are thinking about tying the knot while you're here there are plenty of places to do it. There are more than a dozen chapels in town, ranging from white Victorian churches encrusted in gingerbread trim to log cabin chapels in the woods. You can call 865/453-5502 for information about obtaining a Tennessee marriage license. You can also browse the many chapel options in town with the help of the Gatlinburg Wedding Chapel Association (www.gatlinburgweddingassociation.com).

want to cover the studio tour in its entirety, allow a full day.

Among the shops here is **Licklog Hollow Baskets** (1360 E. Parkway, 865/436-3823, daily 10 A.M.–5 P.M.), where owners Billie and Lisa Canfield sell many of their own creations, including baskets and ironwork. Lisa used her basket-weaving art to help pay for college, but then ended up pursuing it as a career. Other artisans, like David Ogle, owner of **Ogle's Broom Shop** (680 Glades Rd., 865/430-4402, Mon.–Sat. 10 A.M.–5 P.M.), have been part of the cultural landscape of these mountains as long as they can remember. David and his wife, Tammi, are third generation broom makers, David's grandfather having run the shop in the 1940s. A fourth-generation Appalachian chair maker can be found at **The Chair Shop** (830 Glades Rd., 865/436-7413, Mon.–Fri. 9 A.M.–5 P.M., Sat. 10 A.M.–4 P.M.). At the **Paul Murray Gallery** (1003 Glades Rd., 865/436-8445, www.paulmurray.com, Dec.–Mar. Mon.–Sat. 11 A.M.–4 P.M., Apr.–June Mon.–Sat. 11 A.M.–5 P.M., July–Sept. Mon.–Sat. 11 A.M.–6 P.M., Oct.–Nov. daily 11 A.M.–6 P.M.), Canadian-born painter Murray displays his moving portraits of residents of the

mountains of Kentucky and Tennessee. An especially popular stop on the loop tour of the community is **Alewine Pottery** (623 Glades Rd., 866/469-7687, www.alewinepottery.net, daily 9 A.M.–5 P.M.). Master potter Robert Alewine and his students make all the pottery available for purchase here, and you can usually watch them at work. You'll be amazed by the intricate leaf patterns and dazzling colors Alewine creates here in clay. A maple leaf on a vase looks as real here as one you might pick off the forest floor.

At **Otto Preske – Artist in Wood** (535 Buckhorn Rd., 865/436-5339), you can meet someone who has been part of the Great Smoky Arts and Crafts Community for more than a quarter of a century. Preske carves custom wooden mantelpieces with forest scenes of deer and elk, portraits of the persona of the west wind, and long-ago Indian warriors using traditional wood-carving tools. At the **Turtle Hollow Gallery** (248 Buckhorn Rd., 865/436-6188, Mar.–Dec. daily 10 A.M.–6 P.M., Jan.–Feb. Thurs.–Sat. 10 A.M.–6 P.M.), see the works of sculptor Ross Markeley, who has lived and worked in Gatlinburg for 17 years. He carves animals, humans, and unusual sculptures of human body parts in limestone, bronze, marble, and wood.

The Village

A quaint little retail haven in the center of downtown Gatlinburg is The Village (634 Parkway, 865/436-3995, www.thevillage-shops.com) with its fountain and Bavarian-style shops, most of which offer a more upscale atmosphere than the rest of the main drag through town. The Village, which curls away into its own little courtyard away from the main street through town, actually developed because the owners who purchased the property in 1965 were not quite sure what to do with it, having only 24 feet of frontage on the Parkway. The concept of The Village developed as a way to draw people from the main street back into a cozy gathering of shops that might otherwise have been no more than an alleyway.

The concept has worked. More than two dozen specialty shops and cafés now occupy The Village. One of my favorites is **Smoky Mountain Babies** (865/430-9550, Mar.–Nov. daily 10 A.M.–10 P.M., winter hours may vary), which carries high-end baby clothes and toys. If you're in the market for deck shoes, river sandals, or hiking boots to ensure your readiness for outdoor adventure, then check out **The Hayloft-Comfort Shoes** (800/245-2668, daily 10 A.M.–10 P.M.). **The Silver Tree** (865/430-3573, daily 10 A.M.–10 P.M.) is a whole store dedicated to silver jewelry, while **Simply Animals** (865/436-5849, daily 10 A.M.–10 P.M.) carries clothing, collars, toys, and treats for pets—you're welcome to bring in your pooch as well. Early risers can come by **The Donut Friar** (865/436-7306, daily 5 A.M.–10 P.M.) for fresh donuts, pastries, bread, lattes, and cappuccinos. You don't have to get there by 5 A.M., but don't wait too long—the donuts often sell out. If you happen to just be walking by, the smell is almost impossible to resist.

Winter hours for all the shops in The Village are speculative at best. Stores there are not required to have set hours from mid-December to March and will modify their schedule based

The Village in Gatlinburg

on customer traffic, weather, or whim. The weekends are your best bet in the winter.

Downtown Galleries

The Arrowcraft Gallery (576 Parkway, 865/436-4604, www.craftguild.org, May–Nov. Mon.–Sat. 10 A.M.–8 P.M., Sun. 10 A.M.–6 P.M., Dec.–Apr. Mon.–Sat. 10 A.M.–6 P.M., Sun. 10 A.M.–6 P.M.) is one of the most beautiful shops in town, located next to traffic light #6 across from River Road. One of four galleries of the Southern Highland Craft Guild that can be found in the southern mountains, Arrowcraft carries the handmade crafts of guild members, including beautifully turned wooden bowls, blown glass ornaments that sparkle like Christmas lights in the window, handmade jewelry, woven coverlets and table linens, and lovingly crafted toys.

Beneath the Smoke (467 Parkway, 865/436-3460, www.kenjenkins.com, Apr.–Dec. Mon.–Sat. 10 A.M.–8 P.M., Jan.–Mar. 10 A.M.–6 P.M., winter hours may vary) is the gallery of award-winning internationally known photographer and Gatlinburg native Ken Jenkins. The two-story gallery features hundreds of Jenkins' wildlife and landscape photographs from North America and around the world. Allow yourself some time to explore the gallery and peruse Jenkins' moving portraits of black bears, cougars, and eagles as well as his vibrant pictures of some of America's most treasured landscapes from the peaks of the Smokies to the sand and wind-carved rockscapes of the southwestern United States.

Downtown Gifts

Jonathan's (733 Parkway, 877/218-0442, Apr.–Dec. daily 9 A.M.–11 P.M., Jan.–Mar. daily 9 A.M.–8 P.M.) is tucked in among a horde of typical tourist traps on Gatlinburg's main drag right in the midst of the busiest section of the Parkway. The store has a nice selection of casual resort clothing as well as hiking boots, Minnetonka moccasins, and Life is Good clothing and gear, as well as gifts for children.

Maples' Tree (639 Parkway, 800/598-0908, www.maplestree.com, daily 9 A.M.–11 P.M., winter hours may vary) is just down the street and carries factory-made quilts, quilted purses, comfy nightwear for kids and adults, Jim Shore figurines and ornaments, and some home decor and garden items.

ENTERTAINMENT AND EVENTS
Annual Wildflower Pilgrimage

Gatlinburg's Annual Wildflower Pilgrimage (865/436-7318 ext. 222, seminars and classes $10–50) occurs each year across four days in April. During the festival the Great Smoky Mountains National Park offers more than 170 different programs to celebrate the arrival of spring blossoms, including guided hikes, motorcades, lectures, and outdoor programs.

Gatlinburg Fine Arts Festival

Gatlinburg Fine Arts Festival (888/240-1358, www.gfaf.net, free) occurs the third weekend in May and features a juried art show with participating artists from all over the country, as well as live music and food vendors. The fair is held at Ripley's Aquarium and along River Road.

Gatlinburg Craftsmen's Fair

The Gatlinburg Craftsmen's Fair (303 Reagan Dr., 865/436-7479, www.craftsmenfair.com, adults $6, 12 and under free) occurs twice annually during a week in July and then two weeks in October at the Gatlinburg Convention Center. The fair has been going strong for more than three decades and features some 200 craft demonstrators in pottery, woodworking, jewelry making, painting, leather work, and basket weaving from all over the southern Appalachians. Not only do they offer their handmade wares for sale, but most of the artisans demonstrate their craft throughout the day. As part of the festivities, regional musicians fill the convention center with the sounds of dulcimer, banjo, and fiddle. Call or check the website for the current year's dates.

Gatlinburg Winter Magic

Gatlinburg Winter Magic (800/568-4748, www.gatlinburgwintermagic.com) runs from mid-November through February each year. The event kicks off in early November with a chili cook-off and the illumination of the city with over three million twinkling lights, all of them LED bulbs. The last weekend in November, the streets of town are filled with storytellers and carolers for Tunes & Tales, while the Gatlinburg Convention Center is decorated with dozens of Christmas trees. The Fantasy of Lights Christmas Parade occurs the first Saturday of December. What makes the parade particularly unique is that it occurs at night, turning the Parkway through the town center into a moving and rolling spectacle of lights.

SPORTS AND RECREATION
◖ Ober Gatlinburg

Ober Gatlinburg (1001 Parkway, 800/251-9202, www.obergatlinburg.com, daily

10 A.M.–7 P.M., single-session lift tickets $15–47, two-session lift tickets $52–89) is a mountaintop resort overlooking Gatlinburg that offers skiing on eight slopes; there are also 10 lanes for snow tubing with a 50-foot vertical drop. Skiing is typically available mid-December to early March. Ober Gatlinburg also has a year-round indoor ice skating rink in the center of the resort's mall. The resort is open year-round except for a maintenance shutdown of about one week, usually in the spring. Hours of operation are extended in the summer and during ski season, sometimes as late as midnight to accommodate night skiing. The biggest attraction here outside of ski season is the 120-passenger aerial tramway—the largest in the United States—that takes visitors from downtown Gatlinburg to the top of Mount Harrison at 2,700 feet. Ober Gatlinburg also has an 1,800-foot alpine slide that simulates a bobsled ride, offering a ride down the ski trails and through the woods.

Among the warm-weather attractions here are water slides, scenic chair lifts, musical entertainment, and a wildlife exhibit. The Ober Gatlinburg Restaurant and Lounge offers dining with long-distance views, and there are also several snack bars and cafés at the mall.

Just a warning, though—the resort is on the cheesy side, so unless you're coming here to ski, you might want to skip it. Even if you're not interested in visiting the amusement park, however, you might still want to purchase a tramway ticket, as the 10-minute ride up the mountain from downtown offers stunning views of Mount LeConte. The cost to ride the tramway only is $10 for adults and $8.50 for children. If you don't take the tramway, you can access the resort by taking Ski Mountain Road at traffic light #10.

White-Water Rafting

The Pigeon River, which flows along I-40 in the Cherokee National Forest just north of the Great Smoky Mountains National Park, is a great place to test your white-water mettle. Rapids here are mostly Class I to III with a handful of Class IV thrown in to whet your whistle for bigger water in the future, so it's a good rafting location for families and beginners on the water. Most local outfitters cover a five-mile stretch of river around Waterville by I-40 Exit 451. The scenery along this route is lovely with several calm water spots. Rhododendron, dogwoods, redbuds, pears, maples, and oaks create a canopy over the gorge, where an occasional Canadian goose or river otter sidles by.

There are about a dozen local outfitters that offer white-water rafting on the Pigeon River. Among them is **Rafting in the Smokies** (247 E. Parkway, 865/436-5008, www.raftinginthesmokies.com, June–Aug. Tues.–Thurs. and Sat. from 11 A.M., $35–39)—their guides are great. Rafting may also be offered on Sunday, Monday, and Friday and later than Labor Day, dependent on conditions. Call ahead for availability and reservations (required). Once your trip is scheduled, check in at their outpost in Hartford at Exit 447 off I-40.

Nantahala Outdoors Center's Great Outpost (888/905-7238, www.noc.com) is adjacent to the national park entrance on the southern edge of Gatlinburg. NOC is seeking LEED (Leadership in Energy and Environmental Design) certification from the U.S. Green Building Council for the renovated structure it is occupying. The already regionally well-known outfitter provides white-water rafting, kayaking, and float trips on seven area rivers, including the Pigeon River. NOC's Great Outpost also offers guided fly-fishing trips, guided hikes, mountain biking, and outdoor education classes and nature tours.

Other outfitters include **Smoky Mountain Outdoors** (453 Brookside Village Way, 800/771-7238, www.smokymountainrafting.com), which offers white-water and float trips and funyak rentals.

Zip Line

Zip Gatlinburg (905 River Rd., 877/494-7386, www.zipgatlinburg.com, daily 10 A.M.–8 P.M., $50–75) offers a canopy tour featuring nine cables, seven swinging platforms, and two sky bridges. Call or check website booking calendar for available tour times. Reservations can be made online.

Hummer Tours

Off Road Voyages (175 Parkway, 866/998-6924, www.offroadvoyages.com, daily 10 A.M.–4 P.M., $42–75) offers military Hummer (as in Humvee) tours of the Smokies, taking passengers on wild rides up steep mountainsides, through slushy ravines, up 30-degree side slopes, and across creeks to explore the Smoky Mountains on a wild and bumpy ride. This isn't for everyone, especially if you don't like your teeth knocking together, but if you're not into hiking this might be one avenue of experiencing the woods outside the confines of an air-conditioned automobile. Off Road also offers white-water packages in conjunction with Hummer tours.

If you want to rent your own Hummer or a Jeep for exploring on your own, check out **Southland Car and Jeep Rentals** (1011 E. Parkway, 865/436-9811, www.southlandcarjeeprental.com, Apr.–Oct. daily 8 A.M.–8 P.M., Nov.–Mar. Mon.–Sat. 9 A.M.–6 P.M.).

ACCOMMODATIONS

It would be pretty hard not to find a place to stay in Gatlinburg. The town has 12,000 rooms available, and on any given night some 45,000 tourists are spending the night here. And that's in a town where the resident population numbers only 3,500. Unfortunately, the sheer number of choices makes it difficult to sort the good lodgings from the bad. That being said, if you like being close to the action there are dozens of hotels right in town, some with rooms overlooking the busy Parkway, and others a block or so off the main street that provide easy access to attractions and shopping without the associated noise. And keep in mind that, no matter the season, downtown Gatlinburg will be going strong till midnight. Because Gatlinburg enjoys frontage on several rivers and streams pouring down out of the Smokies, even some of the most basic hotels

offer accommodations with stream-front balconies. If you plan to stay in town for several days or a week you might consider a vacation rental, of which there are thousands, to give you more bang for your buck. Many cabins and houses in the area rent by the week, offering you a better deal than the usual nightly charge. If serenity and luxury is what you're seeking, your best bet is probably one of about half a dozen bed-and-breakfasts occupying the curling back roads just outside of town.

Hotels

There are hotels of all descriptions in Gatlinburg, and pretty much all the major chains are represented here somewhere, including Best Western, Super 8, Hampton Inn, Sleep Inn, Days Inn, Clarion, and Comfort Inn as well as dozens of privately owned hotels. If you want to be guaranteed clean, comfortable rooms with reliable service, then your best bet is to reserve at one of the high-end chains, but there are plenty of local operations that are nice. Among them is the **Bearskin Lodge** (840 River Rd., 865/430-4330, www.thebearskinlodge.com, rooms $70–140, suites $110–170), a good hotel for families. It's within walking distance of Gatlinburg's attractions, shopping, and dining but not on the main drag through town, giving it a pretty quiet location. Bearskin Lodge is located on the West Fork of the Little Pigeon River, and many of the rooms have private balconies overlooking the water. Request a room on the west end corner of the hotel for the most privacy (so you're not looking across the river into someone else's hotel room) and for the largest suites with fireplaces and king beds. Kids and tired parents will love this place because it has both an outdoor heated pool and a lazy river that's wonderful to float around in an inner tube after a long day of hiking. There are also two gas fire pits in the pool area where you can roast marshmallows. There are a couple of drawbacks to this place, however: The staff can be downright careless and not particularly interested in the happiness of their guests (a fact of life in way too many accommodations in the area), and while the rooms are clean and orderly they are starting to show some wear. The Bearksin offers complimentary high-speed Internet access as well as continental breakfast.

Opened in 2009, **Hilton Garden Inn** (625 River Rd., 865/436-0048, www.gatlinburg.hgi.com, rooms $109–159, suites $149–169) is the first hotel in the state of Tennessee with LEED (Leadership in Energy and Environmental Design) certification. The green features that will be most readily apparent to guests are the hotel's use of compact fluorescent lightbulbs; motion detectors that turn room lights on and off; low-flow toilets, faucets, and showers; and recycling baskets in guest rooms. The five-story hotel has 112 rooms, each featuring the luxurious Garden Sleep System bed, complimentary Wi-Fi, and complimentary remote printing from guest rooms. The hotel has an outdoor swimming pool, a fitness center, and Stay Fit Kits where guests can check out supplies for yoga and pilates. On-site is a restaurant offering breakfast and dinner as well as all-day room service and a lounge bar.

Fairfield Inn and Suites (168 Parkway, 865/430-3659, www.marriott.com/gtlno, $59–169) is another good family hotel. Though located on the western edge of downtown and not really within easy walking distance of most shopping and restaurants, the hotel does have a trolley stop. Renovated in 2009, the hotel is crisp and new and features a beautiful pool with fountain and waterslide as well as an indoor pool and hot tub. The kids will love that it's right next door to mini-golf. Free continental breakfast is available each morning, and guests enjoy complimentary high-speed Internet access.

Westgate Smoky Mountain Resort and Spa (915 Westgate Resort Rd., 877/819-4028, www.wgsmokymountains.com, 1-bedroom suites $79–159, 2-bedroom suites $149–209, 3-bedroom suites $179–259) is a welcome bit of seclusion that is still convenient to both Gatlinburg and Pigeon Forge. The 70-acre resort has everything you need, from the Wild Bear Falls Waterpark to a hot stone massage at the Serenity Spa. Other amenities include a 24-hour fitness center, two heated pools, and an on-site restaurant and lounge.

Inns and Bed-and-Breakfasts

The **C Timber Rose English Lodge** (1106 Tanrac Trail, 877/235-4993, www.timber-rose.com, $99–159) is located within the Great Smoky Arts and Crafts Community. It was built to resemble an English estate lodge, and the Timber Rose's rambling, ornate architecture and garden cherubs initially seem at odds with the rustic mountain environment around it, but once you step out onto one of the private verandas that grace each of the lodge's five suites the Timber Rose seems perfectly placed. The northeastern view is one of rolling blue ridge after rolling blue ridge. The rooms here are almost as stunning as the view. Decorated in Victorian-era antiques with wood-burning fireplaces and flower-papered walls, they offer an Old World feel complimented by modern amenities—outdoor hot tubs, fully equipped kitchens, and spacious bathrooms. This is a couples-only lodge, and no breakfast is served. However, the suites' fully equipped kitchens provide cookware and utensils for making your own meals. No smoking is permitted indoors.

Also located in the midst of the Great Smoky Arts and Crafts Community, the **Buckhorn Inn** (2140 Tudor Mountain Rd., 866/941-0460, www.buckhorninn.com, rooms $175, cottages $170, guesthouses $195–320) has been welcoming guests since 1938. Nestled in woods and rhododendron stands, the inn overlooks the national park with long views of Mount LeConte, toasty fires, and lazy hammocks under the trees. The Buckhorn also offers dinner on-site. Lodge rooms are elegant, but the cottages' decor (and housekeeping) tends to be a bit on the shabby side, so opt for a lodge room if you can. Two-bedroom guesthouses are also available.

C The Lodge at Buckberry Creek (961 Campbell Lead Rd., 866/305-6343, www.buckberrylodge.com, lodge suites $180–265, gallery suites $225–325, grand suites $300–460) is situated above the town of Gatlinburg and is accessible via Ski Mountain Road.

Featuring what it terms as "camp-style suites," the lodge is anything but rustic, save for its decor. Here the crown moldings are made of cherry and birch with the bark still intact, and rooms are decorated in Adirondack-style furniture. Many of the suites feature views of Mount LeConte from their private verandas. The Lodge at Buckberry Creek is located on 26 private acres adjacent to the Great Smoky Mountains National Park on land that has belonged to the local McLean family for three generations. With its own trout fishing stream, hiking trails, and dining, Buckberry Creek offers enough amenities that guests just seeking a peaceful getaway could spend their entire visit on-site. The service is impeccable, and the staff really knows how to make you feel as if you are the most important person on earth.

Christopher Place Resort (1500 Pinnacles Way, 800/595-9441, www.christopherplace. com, rooms $165, suites $275–330, guest-house $275) is a good place to lay your head if you're looking for a luxury bed-and-break-fast far from the more trammeled areas of the Smokies. Located about 15 miles from the Cosby entrance to the national park off Highway 32 south of Newport, Christopher Place seems like it's in the middle of nowhere, especially as you make the circuitous climb up English Mountain to the resort prop-erty. Once you arrive, you'll understand. The mansion house affords sweeping views of the Smokies to the east and has two long and broad verandas for taking in the scene. Christopher Place occupies 280 acres and has nine guest rooms and suites as well as a guesthouse. The inn features a grand spiraling staircase in the entranceway lighted by a crys-tal chandelier, and the curling stairway will lead you three stories up to the guest game room with pool table, guest fridge, and freshly baked cookies on the bar. The home is deco-rated with family antiques and memorabilia. The current owners had grandparents serv-ing under the Kennedy and Johnson admin-istration, and many historic photos of the era line the walls of the game room. Christopher Place offers dinner on-site with a changing menu. Dinner is served nightly at 7 P.M. and costs $40 per person. The public is welcome with advance reservations. The resort also has an English-library pub where you can order drinks as well as fish-and-chips or beer-boiled

© FRENCH C. GRIMES

Christopher Place Resort

shrimp cocktail. A three-course breakfast is served each morning overlooking the grand eastern view. The inn provides concierge services, including arranging white-water rafting, horseback riding, and guided fly-fishing in the Smokies.

Cabins

There are thousands of cabins and vacation rentals in and immediately around Gatlinburg, and since this is the "wedding capital of the South" many of the rentals cater to couples. Accommodations range from luxurious and tasteful to downright cheesy (think heart-shaped whirlpool tubs). The process of finding the right cabin can be overwhelming with so many offerings.

Be sure to get a clear understanding from the vacation rental operator as to how private your accommodations will be. Many of the city's rental agencies have dozens of cabins grouped together in relatively small spaces, which can quickly spoil your vision of a romantic evening in the hot tub with your spouse if you're staring across the deck at another couple doing the same thing right next door. Others can be right in the thick of residential communities, with their attendant children and dogs running around the neighborhood and local baseball parks shining their lights in your windows till midnight.

Mountain Rentals of Gatlinburg (209 Cartertown Rd., 866/482-1044, www.mountainchalets.com, 1-bedroom $75–145, 2-bedroom $85–200, 3-bedroom $95–165, 4-bedroom $125–275, 5 or more bedrooms $150–575) offers a variety of vacation rental properties. Some of the best options feature private porches with hot tubs, lofts with pool tables, gas fireplaces, full kitchens, and two master suites with whirlpool tubs and king-size beds, all in the same cabin.

Jackson Mountain Homes (1662 E. Parkway, 865/436-8876, www.jacksonmountain.com, 1-bedroom $110–205, 2-bedroom $120–240, 3-bedroom $130–315, 4-bedroom $215–675, 5-bedroom $275–640, 6-bedroom $500–675, 8-bedroom $575–1,100)

has vacation rentals all over Gatlinburg with a rental office on the outskirts of town on Highway 321 north. Many of the cabins feature multiple master-bedroom suites, pool tables, air hockey, hot tubs, gas log fireplaces, and multi-level decks. Rentals are consistently clean, outfitted with high-quality furniture, and armed with security systems to protect valuables. The staff at Jackson Mountain Homes is service-oriented, allowing for quick and easy check-in, including after-hours check-in.

Mountain Laurel Chalets (440 Ski Mountain Rd., 800/626-3431, www.mtnlaurelchalets.com, 1-bedroom $95–195, 2-bedroom $100–229, 3-bedroom $140–300, 4-bedroom $210–315, 5-bedroom $195–350, 6-bedroom $200–450, 7 to 12 bedrooms $400–1,000) seems to have the corner on the market when it comes to high-elevation vacation rentals overlooking Gatlinburg and the Great Smoky Mountains National Park from the twisting back roads accessible off Ski Mountain Road at traffic light #10, such as the three-story chalet I enjoyed, situated with a postcard-perfect view of Mount LeConte from its rear deck with hot tub. As with most vacation rentals in Gatlinburg, Mountain Laurel's homes are privately owned and individually decorated, though common amenities include multiple master suites, full kitchens, gas log fireplaces, hot tubs, and easy check-in procedures. All units are protected by alarmed security systems.

Camping

Twin Creek RV Resort (1202 E. Parkway, 800/252-8077, www.twincreekrvresort.com, Mar.–Nov., $60) is something of a luxury camping resort with 85 paved sites, heated pool and kiddie pool, hot tub, laundry, full hookups, laundry, Wi-Fi, cable TV, bathhouse, playground, decks at every campsite, and access to trolley service. The resort is north of Gatlinburg on Highway 321.

Camping in the Smokies Gatlinburg RV Park (1640 E. Parkway, 865/430-3594, $30–42) is also located on Highway 321 north of Gatlinburg right next door to Gatlinburg City

Hall. Situated along a stream with the national park behind it and shady sites, the resort offers full hookups, cable TV, laundry, bathhouse, and pool. There is trolley service to the campground.

Cosby Campground (127 Cosby Park Rd., 865/436-1200, www.nps.gov/grsm, $14) is located inside the Great Smoky Mountains National Park just inside the Cosby entrance to the park off Highway 321. This is one of the lesser-used national park campgrounds and is a great place to camp if you prefer to get away from the crowds you'll often find in other park campgrounds during periods of peak visitation. Located alongside Cosby Creek, the campground provides access to several hiking trails, including the Gabe Mountain Trail, which leads to Hen Wallow Falls.

FOOD
Casual Fine Dining
Great food can be a little tricky to find in Gatlinburg if you don't know where to look. Too many of the restaurants here, recognizing the fact that most of their customers are tourists and not locals, don't bother to go the extra mile to win back your service as second time. There are a few exceptions, however, and strangely enough, they tend to be owned by the same people, so obviously there are a few restaurateurs in town who know what they're doing.

❰ The Peddler (820 River Rd., 865/436-5794, www.peddlergatlinburg.com, Sun.–Fri. 5 P.M.–close, Sat. 4:30 P.M.–close, $19–38) is a local and tourist favorite and always packed to the gills. The restaurant has lovely riverside seating available in both the dining room and the bar, but unless you get there early your chances of getting one of those coveted tables are slim to none. The Peddler is best known for its steaks, though the charbroiled shrimp is darn good as well. All entrées come with unlimited access to a well-stocked salad bar, and there is a full bar available. The Peddler does not accept reservations but does allow guests to call ahead, so you can get your name on the waiting list before you head to the restaurant.

Bennett's Pit Bar-B-Que (714 River Rd., 865/436-2400, www.bennetts-bbq. com, Sun.–Thurs. 8 A.M.–10 P.M., Fri.–Sat. 8 A.M.–11 P.M., $5–22) is known, of course, for its hickory-smoked barbecue beef, pork, and chicken and gargantuan platters of food. This is southern-style cooking at its dripping best. The restaurant also has a soup and salad bar and breakfast buffet.

The Park Grill (1110 Parkway, 865/436-2300, www.parkgrillgatlinburg.com, Sun.–Fri. 5 P.M.–close, Sat. 4:30 P.M.–close, $13–33) is owned and operated by the same folks that run The Peddler, and some of the menu options are similar. The Park Grill, however, offers some great combo meals like prime rib and chicken or filet mignon and shrimp that come with the salad bar, a side, and fresh hot bread. The restaurant's sweet moonshine chicken is another good one to try. For dessert, grab a friend and order the dessert sampler, which comes with Jack Daniel's crème brûlée, berry cobbler, and chocolate cheesecake trufflette.

❰ Howard's Steakhouse (976 Parkway, 865/436-3600, www.howards-gatlinburg.com, Sun.–Thurs. 11 A.M.–10 P.M., Fri.–Sat. 11 A.M.–11 P.M., $13–50) has, hands down, absolutely best steak burgers in town—and perhaps anywhere in the Smokies. They come with heart-attack-on-a-plate toppings like bacon, mounds of cheese, and even ham, but the taste is worth the risk. Howard's also serves up a surprisingly lean and tasty rib eye. The restaurant has a pub-style atmosphere with booths against the windows and a full bar. If the weather is nice, elect to eat on the outdoor patio overlooking the river. If it's evening, you might see some resident raccoons come out to the river to beg for scraps from the diners above. And while there are few places in the Smokies where you can describe the service as excellent, Howard's is an exception. The waitstaff here is attentive almost to a fault. No dirty plate will sit on your table for longer than two seconds.

Best Italian Café & Pizzeria (968 Parkway, 865/430-4090, www.bestitalian. com, Sun.–Thurs. 11 A.M.–10 P.M., Fri.–Sat. 11 A.M.–11 P.M., $11–23) is located right behind Howard's Steakhouse and is best known for its garlic rolls, which are topped with olive oil, garlic, parmesan, and romano cheese. For your main course, definitely try the filet tips linguini with some of the most tender beef tenderloin tips served up with pasta, onions, and green and red peppers.

For reasons that are unclear to me, the food in Gatlinburg tends to get progressively worse the closer you get to the center of the downtown tourist area. One exception to that is **McCutchan's Brass Grill Restaurant** (710 Parkway, 865/436-4345, www.mccutchans-brassgrill.com, daily 11 A.M.–10 P.M., $9–22), a family-friendly place owned by the same folks who operate Howard's Steakhouse, meaning many of the menu offerings are similar, including the to-die-for cordon bleu burger topped with bacon, blue cheese crumbles, and provolone cheese. I like the fact that the kids' menu doesn't sport the usual junk food fare but offers ham-and-swiss and turkey sandwiches as well as steak burgers.

No Way Jose's Cantina (555 Parkway, 865/430-5673, www.nowayjosescantina.com, daily 11:30 A.M.–10 P.M., $5–13) is a fun place to eat across the road from Ripley's Aquarium and offers pleasant seating on the river. The restaurant offers all the usual fare you'd expect from a Mexican restaurant, all of it reliably good. But the thing you have to order before your meal arrives is a basket of chips with the restaurant's homemade salsa. It's so bitingly fresh it tastes like the ingredients came right out of the garden.

Breakfast

C Pancake Pantry (628 Parkway, 865/436-4724, June–Oct. daily 7 A.M.–4 P.M., Nov.–May daily 7 A.M.–3 P.M., $6–10) is a perennial favorite of mine. I've been here a time or two, or three, and I always have to get my favorite dish—the wildberry crepe, which consists of five types of berries in compote stuffed inside three crepes with creamy ricotta cheese and powdered sugar on top. Diners start lining up at the door at 7 A.M., so get here early! But if you're late, don't worry—they serve breakfast until closing time.

Mountain Lodge Restaurant (913 E. Parkway, 865/436-2547, daily 7 A.M.–3 P.M.,

$3–8) is a local's favorite, without very much tourist traffic. It's located on Highway 321 north a fair distance from the downtown tourist area of Gatlinburg. It's easy to see why the locals like it: It's cheap and reliably good. Four people can eat here for under $20. The fare is typical country breakfast—pancakes, omelets, biscuits and gravy, and toast and grits.

Grocery Service

If you're renting a cabin in the Gatlinburg or Pigeon Forge area and don't want to contend with the hassle of grocery shopping to stock the fridge when you get there, **Smoky Mountain Grocery** (877/484-8853, www.smokymountaingrocery.com, $15 per delivery) will do your shopping for you and deliver groceries to your door on arrival or even pre-arrival if you request it. You can order online.

INFORMATION AND SERVICES
Information

Understanding the visitors centers in Gatlinburg is bit of a challenge. The **Gatlinburg Chamber of Commerce** (800-568/4748, www.gatlinburg.com) is located at East Parkway and operates the **Gatlinburg Welcome Center** (Hwy. 441 S., Memorial Day–Oct. daily 8 A.M.–7 P.M., Nov. daily 8 A.M.–5:30 P.M.). The City of Gatlinburg operates the visitors centers in town. The **Parkway Visitor Center** (520 Parkway, daily 10 A.M.–6 P.M.) is located at traffic light #3 in downtown Gatlinburg at the intersection of U.S. 441 and U.S. 321. The **Aquarium Welcome Center** (88 River Rd., daily 9 A.M.–9 P.M.) is located at traffic light #5 on Ripley's Aquarium of the Smokies Plaza.

Emergency Services

Fort Sanders Sevier Medical Center (709 Middle Creek Rd., 865/429-6100, www.fssevier.com) offers 24-hour emergency service. You can also contact the **Gatlinburg Police** (1230 E. Parkway, 865/436-5181) for assistance.

Media

Gatlinburg has its own cable channel,

WGAT-69, which you can tune into from your hotel room. Channel 69 offers 24/7 information on area attractions, events, shopping, and restaurants.

GETTING THERE

The heaviest traveled route into Gatlinburg is from I-40, and this is the route you will likely take if you're coming in from the north or west. Most visitors exit the interstate at U.S. 66 at Exit 407; 66 will feed into U.S. 441 south to Gatlinburg. However, while this is the simplest route, it is also the busiest. An alternate option is to take Exit 435 off I-40 at Knoxville, and follow U.S. 321 to Gatlinburg.

If you've flown into McGhee-Tyson Airport outside Knoxville, then your best bet is to avoid Knoxville altogether and head south on Highway 129 to Maryville. At Maryville, take 321 north to the park entrance at Townsend or to Pigeon Forge, where you will take a right onto U.S. 441 and follow it right into Gatlinburg.

If you're coming in from Asheville and points east, take I-40 west to Exit 443, and follow the Foothills Parkway to Highway 321 south, which leads right into Gatlinburg.

From the Atlanta area and points south, you can reach Gatlinburg by taking I-85 north to I-985 north, and then following I-985 to U.S. 23, which feeds right into Highway 23/441 in North Carolina. Stay on 441 to Cherokee, and drive through the Great Smoky Mountains National Park on the Newfound Gap Road to reach Gatlinburg.

GETTING AROUND
Parking

Parking in Gatlinburg is something close to a nightmare, in large part due to the traffic and the sheer number of people overwhelming what is still very much a small town. The most hassle-free and inexpensive option is to park at one of the two free park-and-ride lots and then take the trolley. The lots are located at the **Gatlinburg Welcome Center on the Spur** (Hwy. 441 S.) and the **City Hall**

Complex (1230 E. Parkway). Also free is the thrill of capturing an elusive space along River Road, which runs parallel to the Parkway along the West Prong of the Pigeon River between Ripley's Aquarium and Ski Mountain Road. The City of Gatlinburg operates two parking garages, **Ripley's Aquarium Garage** (88 River Rd.) and **Fred McMahan Parking Garage** (520 Parkway). Both garages are $1.75 for the first hour, $1 each hour after that, with a maximum daily charge of $6. There are also three municipal lots. The Anna Porter Public Library Lot (237 Bishop La.) and the lot at 303 Reagan Drive both charge a flat rate of $5 all day. Finally, the lot at 366 Parkway charges $0.75 per hour. If you pay to park, stick with these options. There are plenty of private parking lots, but they can get expensive. Guests at in-town hotels should just leave their cars in the hotel lot and walk or ride the trolley.

Gatlinburg Trolley System

The Gatlinburg Trolley (865/436-3897,

Gatlinburg Trolley

© FRENCH C. GRIMES

www.gatlinburgtrolley.org, daily 8 A.M.–midnight, winter Sun.–Thurs. 10 A.M.–6 P.M., Fri.–Sat. 10 A.M.–10 P.M., $0.50–1) provides access to all of the attractions of Gatlinburg and neighboring Pigeon Forge without the headache of finding parking. The trolleys make frequent stops at clearly marked shelters and stops in Gatlinburg as well as Pigeon Forge. There are 100 trolley stops in Gatlinburg alone. Key stops include the Gatlinburg Welcome Center, where you can park free and ride, as well as the Aquarium Trolley Stop. Special trolley routes also offer tours of the Great Smoky Mountains National Park, trips to Dollywood, and loops around the Great Smoky Arts and Crafts Community. Exact change is required. An interesting side note is that Gatlinburg's 20-trolley fleet is powered by a mixture of B20 biodiesel.

Pigeon Forge and Sevierville

Sevierville is the birthplace of country music legend Dolly Parton. It was here that Parton grew up with her 11 brothers and sisters, some of whom she adopted as her own as she grew into fame. A statue of Dolly, sculpted by well-known local artist Jim Gray, stands in front of the Sevierville Courthouse. The courthouse lawn is one of the few areas of town that still looks as it must have when Parton was growing up here. The rest of Sevierville and its next-door neighbor Pigeon Forge have become booming tourist destinations with over 11 million visitors each year. You may feel, when you arrive here, that all 11 million of those people have decided to come at the same time you have, but it's an illusion. The neon lights and gargantuan attractions that line the roadsides can easily make any visitor feel overwhelmed.

Pigeon Forge has perhaps rightfully earned its reputation as one of the East Coast's biggest tourist traps. If you have kids who need constant entertainment, from go-cart rides to bungee jumping, you'll have no problem finding what they crave. But if you're seeking access to some real culture, you'll have to look a little harder. Surprisingly, one of the best places to find it is Dollywood, an extremely well-designed amusement park with some first-rate country and bluegrass shows and genuine Appalachian crafters displaying their skills and wares.

The town of Pigeon Forge traces the origin of at least part of its name to 1820, when pioneer Isaac Love set up an iron forge here. His son went on to build a tub mill a decade later. That mill is now a National Historic Site, which you can visit at Old Mill Square on the Little Pigeon River. The mill continues to produce flour and cornmeal for use at local restaurants and for sale to the public.

Believe it or not, early settlers here found huge numbers of passenger pigeons along the banks of the Little Pigeon River, feeding on the nuts of the beech trees that bowed over the stream. Thus, Pigeon Forge found its name. But Pigeon Forge and Sevierville both remained quiet rural communities until the Great Smoky Mountains National Park was established here in 1934. Slowly, tourism had its effect on the area, and Pigeon Forge was formally incorporated in 1961.

With the opening of the amusement park that would eventually become Dollywood and the arrival of the World's Fair in neighboring Knoxville in 1982, awareness of eastern Tennessee as a tourist destination increased dramatically. But even though the town looks big with all its visitor services and attractions, its year-round resident population remains relatively small. Just over 6,000 people call Pigeon Forge home.

SIGHTS
◖ Dollywood

Visitors just might catch a glimpse of Dolly Parton at Dollywood (1020 Dollywood Lane,

Pigeon Forge, 865/428-9488, www.dollywood.com, Apr.–Dec., $42–54), where she performs for the amusement park's opening for the season each April. Parton started the theme park in Pigeon Forge more than 20 years ago, and it has since become the town's premier attraction. But this isn't your average theme park. Dollywood has the look of an old-time Appalachian village and small southern town all at the same time with tree-lined streets, ponds, and streams. Rides are tucked into the woods, hardly noticeable, and snack stands sell delightful treats.

And while Dollywood may be best known for Showstreet, where theaters offer up everything from bluegrass and country to square dancing, the park also employs several master craftsmen, honoring the Appalachian arts that Dolly knew as a child. In addition to candle making, blacksmithing, and wood crafting, the park also has its own wagon-making facility known as Valley Carriage Works.

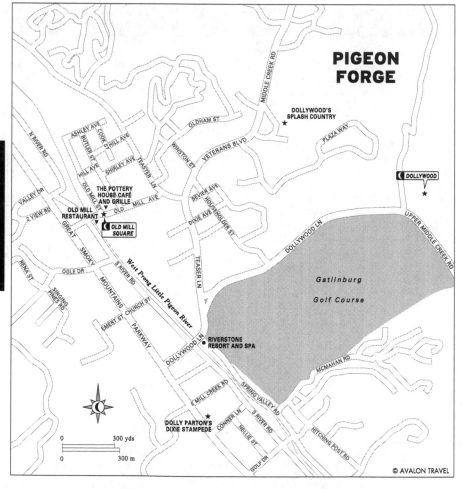

© FRENCH C. GRIMES

Valley Carriage Works at Dollywood in Pigeon Forge

The carriage shop takes actual orders for wagons and carriages and, in fact, built a replica Cherokee wagon to commemorate the 165th anniversary of the Trail of Tears. The wagon is currently on display at the Museum of the Cherokee Indian in Cherokee, North Carolina, and sports an 1838 one-cent piece inserted in the wood in honor of the year in which the Trail of Tears began. Normally, all Valley Carriage Works wagons and carriages carry a penny of the year they were built.

Dollywood, in partnership with the American Eagle Foundation, is also home to the largest gathering of non-releasable bald eagles in America accessible to the public. At Eagle Mountain, park visitors can watch the national bird in its native habitat. The eagles on display have been injured and could not survive in the wild, but they find a comfortable home in the trees here at Dollywood, and daily Wings of America shows put visitors in close contact with the birds.

Shows are held in various theaters and outdoor stages all over Dollywood, though most are concentrated along Showstreet. The music celebrates Dolly's bluegrass and country roots, and some of her relatives perform here. *Sha-Kon-O-Hey!* honors the people and culture of the Smokies with eight original songs Parton wrote for the Great Smoky Mountains National Park's 75th anniversary, which occurred in 2009. The Smoky Mountain String Band combines fiddles, bass, and banjo with down-home comedy. *Dolly's Family Reunion* features Parton's uncles and cousins singing some of Parton's own songs. If you'd like some indication of just how good the music is here, Dollywood has earned more Big E Entertainment Awards in recent years than any other amusement park in the world.

There are restaurants and food stands scattered throughout the park, so you'll never go hungry, though the meals can be a little bit pricey, especially considering what you paid to get into the park in the first place. One of my favorite snacks is the fresh berries and cream concoction available from a stand in the

Craftsman's Valley across from the Wings of America theater.

Rides here run the gamut, allowing plenty of fun for kids of all ages with old-time wooden roller coasters, water rides, and a country fair area with less intimidating options for the little ones. SkyZip offers five zip-line crossings through the park. The ride takes about an hour and a half and costs an extra $40. Two other additions to the park's collection of rides are a new steel coaster known as Mystery Mine and a fun one for younger kids and playful adults, River Battle.

Just in case you haven't spent enough money by the time you're getting ready to leave the park, there are loads of gift shops here. If you're looking for a souvenir, stick to the shops in Craftsman's Valley, where you can actually buy locally crafted goods, most of them made right here in the park—from beautiful leather belts to handblown glass.

The nice thing about Dollywood is really the people who work here, however. These are not "I'm just here for the summer" college kids who don't care about your happiness. Most of the staff is made up of retirees who are here to have fun and enjoy making visitors happy. You won't find a friendlier bunch anywhere.

Parking at Dollywood is $8 per vehicle. You can save yourself some cash, however, by parking your car at Old Mill Square and riding the trolley from there to Dollywood for only $0.50. Days and hours of operation vary throughout the season; check the website or call for details.

Dollywood's Splash Country

Dollywood's Splash Country (2146 Middle Creek Rd., Pigeon Forge, 865/428-9488, www.dollywoodssplashcountry.com, May–Sept. daily 10 A.M.–6 P.M.) is one among several water parks in the Sevierville and Pigeon Forge area, but it is easily the largest. The park features a 25,000-square-foot wave pool, 29 wild water slides, a lazy river, 7,500-square-foot leisure pool, and three interactive children's water play areas. There are also, of course, concessions and a gift shop. Check the website for rates.

© FRENCH C. GRIMES

Dolly's Family Reunion stage at Dollywood in Pigeon Forge

Titanic Pigeon Forge

The *Titanic* Pigeon Forge (2134 Parkway, 866/488-5104, www.titanicpigeonforge.com) is not the first replica *Titanic* to show up in a landlocked town. (There is also one in Branson, Missouri.) But this one is bigger—30,000 square feet, in fact—consisting of three decks with 20 galleries containing genuine *Titanic* artifacts salvaged from the famous sinking ocean liner. The museum showcases exact reproductions of the original *Titanic*'s Marconi wireless room, its grand staircase, a first-class suite, and a third-class cabin. On boarding this vessel, anchored in water, you'll receive a boarding pass with the name of a real *Titanic* passenger, and you'll follow their journey through a 90-minute self-guided tour, learning your fate—rescue or death in icy water—at the tour's end. Kids will especially enjoy the mini-decks where they can test their balance against the real-life slope of the ship's decks as she sank into the ocean in 1912.

© FRENCH C. GRIMES

steam engine at Dollywood in Pigeon Forge

Tennessee Museum of Aviation

The Tennessee Museum of Aviation (135 Air Museum Way, Sevierville, 866/286-8738, www.tnairmuseum.org, Jan.–Feb. Mon.–Sat. 10 A.M.–5 P.M., Sun. 1–5 P.M., Mar.–Dec. Mon.–Sat. 10 A.M.–6 P.M., Sun. 1–6 P.M., adults $12.75, seniors $9.75, children 6–12 $6.75, 6 and under free) is located on the grounds of the Gatlinburg Pigeon Forge Airport and features a 35,000-square-foot hangar full of historic aircraft, including two flyable P-47 Thunderbolts and several Russian MiGs on static display. The museum also has exhibits on the history of aviation, and you might get to see an impromptu flight by one of the historic WWII warbirds. The museum has a large gift shop carrying books on aviation, aviation-related toys, posters, prints, aircraft models and kits, insignia, patches, and pins, as well as T-shirts and caps. The museum is also home to Tennessee's Aviation Hall of Fame.

Dolly Parton Statue

Located on the courthouse lawn in downtown Sevierville is a bronze statue of Sevier County's favorite daughter—Dolly Parton. The statue (125 Court Ave.) was sculpted by local artist Jim Gray and unveiled in 1987. It features the legendary songstress seated with her guitar and that big famous smile spreading across her face. The statue is, quite understandably, a popular photo spot.

SHOPPING
Old Mill Square

Pigeon Forge is full of less "touristy" surprises if you know where to look between the wild rides, hotels, and mini-golf courses. One example is **Old Mill Square** (175 Old Mill Ave., Pigeon Forge, 865/428-0771, www.oldmillsquare.com), situated off Pigeon Forge's main strip at traffic light #7 along the Little Pigeon River. This both restored and re-created historic area has a collection of shops showcasing Appalachian crafts as well as stone-ground flour and grains. **The Old Mill & General Store** (865/453-4628, Mon.–Sat.

8:30 A.M.–9 P.M., Sun. 9 A.M.–8 P.M.) is located in an 1830 gristmill that has been in continuous operation for 180 years. The mill produces flour and meal, which is available for purchase along with old-fashioned glass-bottled sodas, candy, and gift items.

My favorite place in Old Mill Square is **Pigeon River Pottery** (865/453-1104, Mon.–Thurs. 9 A.M.–8:30 P.M., Fri.–Sat. 9 A.M.–9 P.M., Sun. 9 A.M.–8 P.M.), where you can actually see potters at work in the studio behind the shop. For a signature souvenir, pick up a member of the potters' Mighty Bear series, a collection of handcrafted bears in various shapes and sizes fired right here in the studio and representative of the Smokies' beloved mascot—the American black bear.

The **Old Mill Toy Bin** (865/774-2258, Sun.–Thurs. 9:30 A.M.–8 P.M., Fri.–Sat. 9 A.M.–9 P.M.) carries a host of both modern and nostalgic toys, from little red wagons to tin tea sets. The **Old Mill Candy Kitchen** (865/453-7516, Mon.–Thurs. 9 A.M.–8:30 P.M., Fri.–Sat. 9 A.M.–9 P.M., Sun. 9 A.M.–8 P.M.) is another fun place to stop, kid or not. Try the chocolate-covered peanut butter–stuffed graham crackers. At **The Farmhouse Kitchen** (865/428-2044, Sun.–Thurs. 9:30 A.M.–8 P.M., Fri.–Sat. 9 A.M.–9 P.M.) you can pick up all kinds of kitchen gadgets as well as sauces and soup mixes, including the mix for the killer loaded-baked-potato soup served at The Pottery House Café and Grille just down the street.

Specialty Stores

The Christmas Place (2470 Parkway, Pigeon Forge, 865/453-0415, www.christmasplace.com, daily 9 A.M.–10 P.M.) bills itself as the South's largest and most beautiful Christmas store. I don't know the truth of either statement, but this place is pretty darn big, rambling through several Bavarian-looking buildings with grounds so coated with blooms in spring and summer that for Christmas to come and spoil the color almost seems a travesty. Whether you're into holiday kitsch or not, this store is worth checking out. In addition to

Christmas decorations by the thousands, you'll also find artificial trees, a custom floral department, candy kitchen, Vera Bradley items, and special toy and ornament galleries for kids.

If you're in the market for cowboy boots, then you definitely need to stop by **Stages Western Wear** (2765 Parkway, Pigeon Forge, 865/453-8086, www.stageswest.com, Mon.–Sat. 9 A.M.–9 P.M.), which has over 9,000 pairs of boots in stock plus everything else you need to complete your Western ensemble.

The **Tanger Outlets** (1645 Parkway, Sevierville, 865/4533-1053, www.tanger-outlet.com, Mon.–Sat. 9 A.M.–9 P.M., Sun. 10 A.M.–7 P.M.) are located at traffic light #13 in Sevierville and feature dozens of outlet shops for brand names like Polo Ralph Lauren, Nautica, J. Crew, Eddie Bauer, Old Navy, and Calvin Klein.

The Apple Barn Cider Mill & General Store (230 Apple Valley Rd., Sevierville, 865/453-9319, www.applebarncidermill.com, May–Oct. Mon.–Thurs. 9 A.M.–7 P.M., Fri.–Sat. 9 A.M.–9 P.M., Sun. 10 A.M.–6 P.M., Nov.–Apr. Mon.–Sat. 9 A.M.–5:30 P.M., Sun. 1–6 P.M.) is located on a working apple orchard just outside Sevierville, and the smell of apples is probably the first thing you'll notice upon entering the store. You can purchase freshly picked apples right off the tree, buy cider and sparkling juice, dive into a fresh-baked apple pie, or browse the country store, which also sells wine, chocolate, smoked ham, local crafts, and old-fashioned candy. The Apple Barn also has an ice cream shop. The working orchard that surrounds the farm has more than 4,000 fruit trees, bearing 14 different kinds of apples. There are two restaurants on-site as well, the Applewood Farmhouse Restaurant and the Applewood Farmhouse Grill.

ENTERTAINMENT AND EVENTS
Entertainment

There are more than a dozen theaters in Pigeon Forge offering musical entertainment, comedy, and even bison stampedes. Their offerings range from some incredibly talented performers to the downright silly, so select your pricey evening entertainment carefully. The best show in town is at the **Country Tonite Theatre** (129 Showplace Blvd., Pigeon Forge, 800/792-4308, www.countrytonitepf.com, $23–28). Don't let the over-the-top glitz fool you—people in this town can actually sing, play…and dance. Country Tonite is a prime example. This show will appeal to just about anyone, country music fan or not. Check out Mike Caldwell's incredible harmonica playing, and the fast and fancy moves of the dancers. Even Bubba the Redneck's Elvis impersonation is good! Shows are at 3 and 8 P.M. daily.

Dolly Parton's Dixie Stampede (3849 Parkway, Pigeon Forge, 800/356-1676, www.dixiestampede.com, daily, call for show times, $42–47) is the most popular show in town, seating 1,000 people for each of five shows a day during peak season. It's almost impossible to describe a dinner theater with charging longhorns—you pretty much have to experience it to believe it. Every show comes with a four-course country-style meal. And among the amazing things you'll see happening in the arena before you are horses jumping through fire, a rodeo competition, charging Yankees and Confederates, lots of cowboys and cowgirls singing and kicking up their heels, and ostrich races. Yes, I said ostrich races. And bison, too. You won't leave the Dixie Stampede hungry or even bored, but you might leave scratching your head at the meaning of it all.

Events

Wilderness Wildlife Week (865/429-7350, www.mypigeonforge.com/wildlife, free) takes place in January and is the town's first major event in a year loaded with more festivals than one can possibly list. This is one of the better ones, however, because it actually involves the great outdoors in a natural way, something that is a bit of an anomaly for this town. The event is headquartered at the Music Road Convention Center. During the week there are more than 175 workshops available, all of them run by experts who can talk about the Smokies' earliest pioneers as well as the area's special flora and fauna. There are art and music classes available as well as 40 guided hikes and field trips in the Great Smoky Mountains National Park. Wilderness Wildlife Week has a musical side, too, with one night devoted to **AppalachiaFest** (800/792-4308, www.mypigeonforge.com/music, adults $15, 17 and under $5) at the Country Tonite Theatre. The event features traditional mountain music, ranging from folk to Celtic, and typically has several award-winning artists—in the past Tim O'Brien and Boogertown Gap have performed. Interestingly enough, these two winter events make Pigeon Forge worth visiting for those, like myself, who tend to shy away from the neon lights, hordes of people, and downright ridiculous attractions that seem to dominate Pigeon Forge most of the rest of the year.

The **Annual Dolly Parade** (865/429-7350, www.mypigeonforge.com/parade) draws more than 60,000 people to Pigeon Forge in April, the main reason being that this is when Sevier County's own Dolly Parton returns to town as grand marshall. The parade usually begins at traffic light #6 and follows the Parkway to traffic light #3. You better arrive early if you want to get a good viewing spot from which to check out one of country music's biggest stars.

Sevierville's Bloomin' Barbeque & Bluegrass (888/889-7415, www.bloomin-bbq.com, free) occurs each May and features the Tennessee State Championship Barbeque Cook-Off as well as free bluegrass concerts, which have in the past featured legends Marty Stuart, Larry Cordle & Lonesome Standard Time, and Doyle Lawson & QuickSilver. There are also kids' games, mountain craft vendors, and, of course, plenty of food. You can also hear the finalists from Sevierville's Mountain Soul Vocal Competition. These folks get to compete not just for a cash prize but for a Nashville recording session. The catch is that participants have to sing one of Sevierville native Dolly Parton's songs in any style—be it country, rock, pop, or even rap!

Winterfest (www.smokymountainwinterfest.com) kicks off in early November each year and extends until February. Over four million Christmas lights make Pigeon Forge brighter than it already is, if you can believe it. Among the light displays are a scene of the Old Mill, lighted snowflakes that seem to fall from the sky, and a 40-foot-tall light monument of the U.S. Marines raising the American flag at Iwo Jima. Live music, street dancing, hayrides with Santa, and lots of hot cocoa can all be found in both Pigeon Forge and Sevierville. Visitors can board the Fun Time Trolley at Patriot Park at 6:30 P.M. Monday through Friday to take a trolley tour of the lights. The fare is $5, and you can make reservations by calling 865/453-6444.

SPORTS AND RECREATION
Zorb
You may have heard of Zorb. Like most off-the-wall, death-defying outdoor recreation experiences, it started in New Zealand. Well, now it has come to Pigeon Forge (a likely spot for sure), and it is here in the Smoky Mountains and nowhere else in North America that you can test your mettle by free-falling downhill in a giant rubber ball. **Zorb Smoky Mountains** (203 Sugar Hollow Rd., Pigeon Forge, 865/428-2422, www.zorb.com/zorb/smoky, daily 9 A.M.–5 P.M., 1 ride $37–44, 3-ride combo $81) just might give you the ride of your life. If you're brave enough to try it, here's what you'll experience: You climb into an 11-foot-tall orb-within-an-orb, and then careen 750 feet downhill. By the time you think you just might die before it's over, the ride is done, and you're thinking it might be a hoot to do it again. The Zorbit ride finds you strapped into a Zorb ball so you repeatedly roll upside down or whichever other way the ball decides to send you. If Zorbit wasn't thrilling enough, you can try out Zydro, which uses the same giant ball and adds water inside with you—and you can go bouncing and sloshing down the hill with two of your closest friends inside.

Indoor Skydiving
Fly Away (3106 Parkway, Pigeon Forge, 877/293-0639, www.flyawayindoorskydiving.com, daily 10 A.M.–7 P.M., 1 flight $32, 5 flights $105, 5-flight coaching package $175) is one of the few indoor skydiving attractions in the United States. The vertical wind tunnel here allows you to defy gravity and "free fly" above the ground. Coaching is available, and even experienced skydivers will find the attraction worthwhile as a chance to practice their freefall skills.

Helicopter Tours
If you have the spare cash, it's quite a spectacle to see the Smoky Mountains from the air as well as get some perspective on the sprawl of Pigeon Forge. **Scenic Helicopter Tours** (2174 Parkway, Pigeon Forge, 865/453-6342, www.flyscenic.com, call for days and hours, $11–467) offers a variety of flights over the region. Flights range from a two-mile introductory flight over Pigeon Forge ($10) to a 100-mile flight over nearly the entire Great Smoky Mountains National Park ($396). If you plan to go, check the website for online booking discounts.

Golf
The **Gatlinburg Golf Course** (520 Dollywood Lane, Pigeon Forge, 800/231-4128, www.golf.gatlinburg-tn.com, daily, call for hours, $30–60) is actually in Pigeon Forge and accessible from Highway 441 at traffic light #8. This scenic course is laid out over a rolling landscape with the peaks of the Smokies rising in the distance. Featuring 18 holes, this Bob Cupp–designed championship layout is best known for the 12th hole, which has been nicknamed Sky Hi because it's 194 yards in length and drops 200 feet from tee to green. The golf clubhouse has a pro shop, locker rooms, and a full-service restaurant.

ACCOMMODATIONS
Hotels and Resorts
Like Gatlinburg, Pigeon Forge and Sevierville have lodging options galore and all the usual chain hotels like Best Western, Days Inn,

Clarion, Fairfield Inn & Suites, and Comfort Inn, but there are a few local standouts if you're actually brave enough to sleep in this town. My favorite is ☾ **The Inn at Christmas Place** (119 Christmas Tree La., Pigeon Forge, 888/465-9644, www.innatchristmasplace.com, rooms $119–189, suites $189–339), located on Pigeon Forge's main drag right across the street from The Incredible Christmas Place, the South's largest Christmas store. It's Christmas all year long at this beautiful turreted hotel, and the kids will love the outdoor pool with 95-foot figure-eight waterslide. The rooms—many of which have balconies overlooking the inn's beautifully landscaped grounds and flower gardens—and common areas of the hotel are all decorated for the holidays, and Christmas music plays all day long. There is an indoor pool available as well, and all guests receive a complimentary continental breakfast.

Riverstone Resort and Spa (212 Dollywood La., Pigeon Forge, 888/908-0908, www.riverstoneresort.com, 1-bedroom $109–159, 2-bedroom $139–209, 3-bedroom $160–239, 4-bedroom $220–310) offers spacious one- to four-bedroom condominiums, all with fireplaces, whirlpool tubs, luxury linens, and flat-panel TVs. Resort guests have access to a beautiful indoor atrium pool, 300-foot lazy river, day spa, fitness center, and children's playground. There is also the 18-hole Gatlinburg Golf and Country Club course next to the resort. No doubt about it—this place is a top-shelf offering. Even though it's right in town, you feel like you're miles away from everything when you reserve a room fronting the river. You don't even know that Pigeon Forge is there behind you.

Vacation Rentals

As with Gatlinburg, navigating the vacation rental market in Pigeon Forge can be a challenge since there are so many offerings. But there are a few standouts that offer consistently good service and amenity-laden options. They include **Accommodations by Sunset Cottage** (3630 S. River Rd., Pigeon Forge, 800/940-3644, www.sunsetcottage.com, 1-bedroom $80–199, 2-bedroom $90–250, 3-bedroom $150–325, 4-bedroom $175–800), which has rentals available ranging from one to eight bedrooms, in condos, cottages, cabins, and mountain chalets. Most rentals have ample porches and decks, fireplaces, hot tubs, Wi-Fi, and pool privileges. Sunset Cottage has over 300 options from which to choose.

Alpine Mountain Village (2519 Sand Pike Blvd, Pigeon Forge, 800/405-7089, www.alpinemountainvillage.com, 1-bedroom $110–220, 2-bedroom $125–275, 3-bedroom $160–495, 4-bedroom $235–460, 5-bedroom $235–460, 6-bedroom $305–725, 7-bedroom $305–725) offers log homes only a quarter mile off the busy Parkway but seemingly worlds away because they're tucked behind a ridge. Some of the homes are luxurious, sprawling residences set up to serve a large family group.

Another excellent local vacation rental provider is **Bluff Mountain Realty and Rentals** (2186 Parkway, Pigeon Forge, 800/462-2134, www.bluffmountainrentals.com, 1-bedroom $90–145, 2-bedroom $120–267, 3-bedroom $210–267, 5-bedroom $350–400, 7-bedroom $490–560). Bluff Mountain rents everything from condos to chalets and has dozens of properties available.

Eagle's Ridge Resort (2740 Florence Dr., Pigeon Forge, 866/450-1965, www.eaglesridge.com, 1-bedroom $114–129, 2-bedroom $139–149, 3-bedroom $164, 4-bedroom $204, 5 to 9 bedrooms $254–624) has one- to nine-bedroom log cabins available, many with fireplaces, hot tubs, pool tables, and Wi-Fi. Guests have access to a swimming pool and clubhouse and are only one mile away from the Parkway in Pigeon Forge.

If you want to be in on the action or just like people-watching, then **Whispering Pines Condominiums** (205 Ogle Dr., Pigeon Forge, 866/454-7150, www.whisperingpinescondos.com, $130–250) is the place to be. You can select from condominiums overlooking the Parkway, giving you front-row bleacher seats on all the activities below, or you can opt for a unit on the back side of the facility with mountain views.

This is a good option for families who need lots of space and are looking for clean and comfortable lodgings without spending a fortune.

Camping

KOA Campground (3122 Veterans Blvd., Pigeon Forge, 865/453-7903, www.pigeonforgekoa.com, campsites $32–50, deluxe sites $75–80, cabins $55–70) is conveniently located near Dollywood and has 175 campsites, a heated pool, hot tub, Wi-Fi, fitness center, game room, playground, and laundry.

River Edge RV Park (4220 Huskey St., Pigeon Forge, 800/477-1205, www.stayriveredge.com, $28–38) has 175 sites, many of them on the Little Pigeon River. The RV park has full hookups, cable, bathhouse, laundry, and is located right next to a Fun Time Trolley stop.

Riverside RV Park (4280 Boyds Creek Hwy., Sevierville, 800/341-7534, www.riversidecamp.com, campsites $28–30, cabins $75–89, mobile home $89) is a scenic campground in Sevierville located on the banks of the Little Pigeon River. They offer 265 shaded campsites with full hookups, cable TV, laundry, pool, on-site general store with LP gas for sale, bathhouses, playground, and an arcade. Campers can fish from the campground, too. They also have rustic cabins and a mobile home for rent.

River Plantation RV Park (1004 Parkway, Sevierville, 800/758-5267, www.riverplantationrv.com, campsites $22–50, cabins $20–74) is located in Sevierville right off Highway 441, making it convenient to all the local attractions. The park has 285 sites and caters to oversized rigs. Sites feature concrete patios, full hookups, central modem hookups as well as Wi-Fi, and cable TV. The campground also has riverfront sites available, as well as cabins. Amenities on-site include three laundries, two pools, three bathhouses, a camp store, and a banquet hall.

FOOD

At **◖ The Pottery House Café and Grille** (3341 Old Mill Ave., Pigeon Forge, 865/453-6002, www.oldmillsquare.com, Sun.–Thurs. 11 A.M.–8 P.M., Fri.–Sat. 11 A.M.–9 P.M., $5–18), located in Pigeon Forge's Old Mill Square kitty-corner across the street from The Old Mill, the food is consistently excellent. One of the best dishes here is the restaurant's signature quiche Lorraine with french onion soup and cinnamon bread with butter. The loaded-baked-potato soup with fresh baked bread is another filling comfort-food option. The soup is thick and creamy with hunks of skin-on potatoes floating and shredded cheese and scallions on top. I also recommend the homemade potato chips as well as the tender and juicy rib-eye steak. The Pottery House Café offers indoor and outdoor seating and serves their fare on dishes made next door at Pigeon River Pottery. Across the street from The Pottery House Café is **The Old Mill Restaurant** (164 Old Mill Ave., Pigeon Forge, 865/429-3463, www.oldmillsquare.com, daily 7:30 A.M.–9 P.M., $5–18), which is a family-friendly place with tables overlooking the Pigeon River. They offer traditional fare like country ham, grits, corn fritters, corn chowder, chicken and dumplings, and southern fried catfish, but, in my opinion, the food is a bit bland, service a bit haphazard, and the atmosphere a little too loud. But some folks just like the experience of eating riverside and getting huge portions of comfort food all in one casual, no-fuss kind of place.

Mama's Farmhouse (208 Pickel St., Pigeon Forge, 865/908-4646, www.mamasfarmhouse.com, daily 8 A.M.–10 P.M., $6–17) is almost like sitting down for a meal at your grandmother's house, and it's not just because of the food. The restaurant is located in a sprawling farmhouse with wide front porches loaded with rocking chairs, and there are even a couple of tractors parked out front. And there is a story behind all this: The restaurant is dedicated to the memory of the owner's great-grandmother, and many of her old-time recipes are cooked up for guests here. This is not your typical country-style restaurant. Meals are served family-style, and there is no menu—you just help yourself from heaping bowls set down on the table in front of you. You can have all you want of Mama's fried chicken, biscuits and cornbread, green beans, corn, mashed potatoes, macaroni-and-cheese—all those deep comfort foods of childhood. The restaurant serves breakfast, lunch, and dinner, and if you stop by for your first meal of the day, be sure to dig into those biscuits drenched in peach butter.

Opened in 2009, **New Orleans on the River** (2430 Winfield Dunn Pkwy., Pigeon Forge, 865/933-7244, www.neworleansontheriver.com, Mon.–Sat. 11 A.M.–2 P.M. and 5–10 P.M., $8–16) is a much needed addition to the Pigeon Forge scene. Atmosphere is hard to find in this town, but New Orleans offers it with window seating providing lovely views of the French Broad River and Louisiana-style cooking that will fire up your taste buds. Some of their offerings include chicken-and-sausage jambalaya served with corn relish and the Creole essential red beans and rice. Before digging into the main course, however, be sure to try the fondue-stuffed tomato, a fried green tomato loaded up with seafood fondue and shrimp. If you want a window seat (which you do!), make reservations in advance.

Mel's Diner (119 Wears Valley Rd., Pigeon Forge, 865/429-2184, www.melsdinerpf.com, daily 7 A.M.–close, $4–11) is a fun place to stop if you'd like to soak up some 1950s atmosphere in a restaurant that has been built to look like a classic diner. Open for breakfast, lunch, and dinner, the diner serves hamburgers piled high with lettuce, cheese, bacon, tomatoes, and onions with a stack of fries on the side, as well as breakfast plates that could probably power you through a whole day without lunch. You can order a variety of omelets sandwiched between hash browns and buttered toast. And, of course, you can order any type of soda fountain concoction you can think of, including banana splits featuring oozing syrups in three flavors and towers of whipped cream.

INFORMATION AND SERVICES
Information
The **Pigeon Forge Welcome Center** (1950 Parkway, Pigeon Forge, 800/251-9100, www.mypigeonforge.com, Mon.–Sat. 8:30 A.M.–5 P.M., Sun. 1–5 P.M.) is located at traffic light #0 on the Parkway (U.S. 441). A second visitors center, the **Pigeon Forge Information Center** (3107 Parkway, 800/251-9100, Mon.–Fri. 8:30 A.M.–5 P.M.), is located at traffic light #5, also on the Parkway.

If you're crazy enough to come into the Smokies by way of ridiculously busy U.S. 66, then the **Sevierville Chamber of Commerce Visitors Center** (3099 Winfield Dunn Pkwy., Sevierville, 888/738-4378, www.visitsevierville.com, Mon.–Sat. 8:30 A.M.–5:30 P.M., Sun. 9 A.M.–6 P.M.) is a good place to stop, not just for information on the Sevierville and Pigeon Forge area but for guidance on visiting Gatlinburg and the Great Smoky Mountains National Park, too. The Sevierville Chamber of Commerce shares space here with the **Sevierville Visitor Center of the Great Smoky Mountains Association** (888/898-9102, www.thegreatsmokymountains.org, daily 9 A.M.–5 P.M.). The national park visitors center also has a gift shop selling books on outdoor recreation, local history, and flora and fauna. The visitors centers are just south of I-40 on Highway 66.

Emergency Services
Fort Sanders Sevier Medical Center (709 Middle Creek Rd., Sevierville, 865/429-6100, www.fssevier.com) offers 24-hour emergency service. From U.S. 441 take Dolly Parton Parkway (U.S. 411) east in Sevierville, travel approximately one mile, and turn right on Middle Creek Road.

If you require police services, there are several options: **Sevier County Sheriff's Office** (106 W. Bruce St., Sevierville, 865/453-4668), **Pigeon Forge Police Department** (225 Pine Mountain Rd., Pigeon Forge, 865/453-9063), **Sevier County Police Department** (300 Gary Wade Blvd., Sevierville, 865/453-5506).

TENNESSEE FOOTHILLS

GETTING THERE

The heaviest traveled route into Pigeon Forge and Sevierville is from I-40, and this is the route you will likely take if you're coming in from the north or west. Most visitors exit the Interstate at U.S. 66 at Exit 407. U.S. 66 goes right into Sevierville and then feeds into U.S. 441 to Pigeon Forge. The two towns merge into one another, so you may not even notice you've passed from one into the other.

If you're coming in from Asheville and points east, take I-40 west to Exit 407, and follow the same route.

From the Atlanta area and points south, you can reach Pigeon Forge by taking I-85 north to I-985 north, and then following I-985 to U.S. 23, which feeds right into Highway 23/441 in North Carolina. Stay on 441 to Cherokee, and drive through the Great Smoky Mountains National Park on the Newfound Gap Road to reach Gatlinburg and then Pigeon Forge and Sevierville.

GETTING AROUND

The **Pigeon Forge Fun Time Trolley** (186 Old Mill Ave., Pigeon Forge, 865/453-6444, www.pigeonforgetrolley.org, Mar.–Oct. daily 8:30 A.M.–midnight, Nov.–Dec. 10 A.M.–10 P.M., $0.50) has more than 100 stops throughout Pigeon Forge, Sevierville, and Gatlinburg, too. The trolleys feature new propane/electric hybrid motors.

Townsend

TENNESSEE FOOTHILLS

Townsend is often referred to as the "quiet side of the Smokies," and if you're not interested in the tourist glitz of Gatlinburg and Pigeon Forge, this would be the best place on the Tennessee side to use as a home base for visiting the Great Smoky Mountains National Park. Townsend is also the closest town to Cades Cove, one of the park's most popular areas, where you can take a loop tour by car or bicycle of a once-thriving Appalachian community in one of the Smokies' most scenic valleys.

SIGHTS

Tuckaleechee Caverns

Tuckaleechee Caverns (825 Cavern Rd., 865/448-2274, www.tuckaleecheecaverns. com, Mar. 15–31 daily 10 A.M.–5 P.M., Apr.–Oct. daily 10 A.M.–6 P.M., Nov. 1–15 daily 10 A.M.–5 P.M., adults $14, children $7) was founded as a commercial cave in 1953 by two boyhood friends who had played in the undeveloped cave as children. Together they worked four years to raise money and also to prepare the cave for guests. Their labor paid off: Shortly after the cave opened to the public, members of the National Speleological Society discovered the Big Room, which at more than 400 feet long, 300 feet across, and 150 feet deep is one of the largest cavern rooms in the eastern United States. You can take a one-mile guided tour to see the Big Room, as well as the lower falls of the 200-foot-high Silver Falls.

Great Smoky Mountains Heritage Center

Great Smoky Mountains Heritage Center (123 Cromwell Dr., 865/448-0044, www.gsmheritagecenter.org, Mon.–Sat. 10 A.M.–5 P.M., Sun. noon–5 P.M., adults $6, seniors $4, children 6–17 $4, under 6 free) is the place to delve into the cultural history of East Tennessee. Exhibits, educational programs, and demonstrations showcase the history of Native Americans in the region as well as pioneer culture. You can visit several historic relocated and reconstructed buildings adjacent to the center to glimpse life as it was a century ago.

Foothills Parkway

If you'd like to enjoy a scenic drive of high-elevation vistas without going into the Great Smoky Mountains National Park, check out the Foothills Parkway. Access to the Parkway is on the left off Highway 321 5.5 miles from Townsend. There are numerous overlooks along this 17-mile stretch of parkway offering views of the western slopes of the Great Smoky Mountains National Park as well as views of the Tennessee Foothills and lakes to the west. If you stop at Look Rock, you can take a half-mile hike to an observation tower from which you'll enjoy 360-degree views.

SPORTS AND RECREATION
Horseback Riding
Davy Crockett's Riding Stables (505 Old Cades Cove Rd., 865/448-6411, www.davycrockettridingstables.com, daily 9 A.M.–5 P.M., 30-minute to two-hour ride $15–40, half day $90, overnight $60) offers rides from a half hour to overnight trips into the surrounding mountains. Rides are first come, first served from March to November, but reservations are required in the off-season; call for further information.

Cades Cove Riding Stables (865/448-9009, www.cadescovestables.com, Mar.–Dec. 9 A.M.–6 P.M., 1-hour guided horseback ride $25, 30-minute guided carriage ride $8, guided hayride $6–8) offers trail rides along a nature trail within the cove for half- and one-hour rides. They also offer half-hour horsedrawn carriage rides through Cades Cove daily. Another option is to take a hayride through the cove. Call for times of carriage and hayrides.

Tours
Cades Cove Heritage Tours (123 Cromwell Dr., 865/448-8838, www.cadescoveheritagetours.org, daily 8:30 A.M.–5 P.M., $10–17) is a chance to leave the driving to someone else. The tour takes you in a 19-passenger van on a guided tour of Cades Cove while expert guides detail the cultural history, little-known stories, and natural beauty of the area. Tours depart Townsend at 1 P.M. daily from the Great Smoky Mountains Heritage Center.

Dual Sport Motorcycle Rentals (8457 Hwy. 73, 865/448-6090, www.gsmmotorent.com, call for days and hours, $75–148) offers

motorcycle rentals as well as guided tours into the park and the Cherokee National Forest. Explore little-traveled areas on both paved and gravel roads on a Kawasaki KLR 650 dual sport bike.

ACCOMMODATIONS
Hotels
Lodge at Valley View (7726 E. Lamar Alexander Pkwy., 800/292-4844, www.valleyviewlodge.com, rooms $45–109, suites $120–300) is a rustic lodge on 15 acres with a lovely setting beneath the Smokies. The lodge offers a variety of accommodations from simple lodge rooms to suites with fireplaces, hot tubs, and private decks. All guests can enjoy the landscaped grounds, two outdoor pools, hot tubs, and a really neat Play Village for the kids. The lodge is located on Townsend's walking and jogging trail, giving you the opportunity to stroll to dinner if you like.

Inns and Bed-and-Breakfasts
Gracehill (1169 Little Round Top Way, 866/448-3070, www.gracehillbandb.com, $250–325) is a gorgeous luxury estate home with floor-to-ceiling windows and 12-foot-high ceilings in many rooms, letting the outdoors in with a bang. The inn's rooms are incredibly spacious, offering decadent bathrooms where windows over the whirlpool tubs look onto the Smokies, antique furnishings, fireplaces, and graceful french doors leading onto private balconies. Guests can enjoy an on-site fitness center and an 80-bush rose garden, as well as breakfast each morning.

Vacation Rentals
Pioneer Cabins (288 Boat Gunnel Rd., 800/621-9751, www.pioneercabins.com, $95–175) are a good option if you plan to stay in the area a few days, want some peace and quiet, and have kids in tow. Located down a country road well off Highway 321 on a small organic farm, Pioneer Cabins offers six cabins for rent, sleeping 4–12 people. The cabins are rustic but offer fully equipped kitchens, lots of space for hanging out, ample front porches with rocking

chairs, wood-burning fireplaces, and hot tubs. The atmosphere is definitely one where you feel like it's okay not to keep a constant eye on the kids. Children will especially love the farm's petting zoo, where they can hang out with horses and donkeys. Many of the cabins, though nestled in the woods, offer lovely cut-out views of the Tennessee Foothills.

Camping

The **Tremont Outdoor Resort** (800/448-6373, www.tremontcamp.com, campsites $24–65, cabins $55–115, log homes $100–175) is the closest campground to the national park entrance at Townsend. Offering campsites with full hookups as well as cabins for rent, the campground is located on 2,000 feet over shady river. The campground also has a pool, camp store, bathhouses, game room, tubing, and river fishing available to guests. There are also log homes, situated on a terraced hillside overlooking the mountains.

Tuckaleechee Campground (7259 E. Lamar Alexander Hwy., 865/448-9608, RV sites $39–42, tent sites $35–37, primitive sites $24) has a variety of camping options, including 50 full hookup RV sites, tent sites with water and electricity, and primitive campsites. There are several shady sites next to the river.

Big Meadow Family Campground (8215 Cedar Creek Rd., 888/497-0625, www.big-meadowcampground.com, $35–45) has full electrical hookups and some sites with concrete pads and patios. On-site is a camp store, exercise room, laundry, bathhouse, and trout fishing. Some sites are right on the river.

Look Rock Campground (Foothills Pkwy., 800/365-2267, $14) is not in Townsend but on the Foothills Parkway 18 miles west of town. This is probably the best National Park Service campground in the Smokies, as it's located high on a ridge (meaning no bugs!) with lovely views. It also tends to be sparsely populated, making it a good place for campers who prefer to enjoy complete peace and quiet, though it is an isolated spot. The campground has 69 sites available on a first-come, first-served basis.

There are no RV hookups. Reservations are not available, but the campground rarely fills up. Make sure to secure your valuables before you leave to go sightseeing for the day.

FOOD

The best place to eat in Townsend is **(Riverstone Family Restaurant** (8511 Hwy. 73, 865/448-8816, $6–18), which not only serves up consistently good southern country fare but also has some surprisingly excellent live musical entertainment nightly from 5:30 to 9 P.M. You'll likely hear some good renditions of songs from Johnny Cash, George Strait, Charlie Pride, and Patsy Kline, and sometimes the diners join in the singing. This is where the locals eat, and you can tell by the full parking lot—always a good sign. The must-try items on their menu are the fried dill pickles, fried green tomatoes, and frog legs. Riverstone makes an excellent cheeseburger marinated in Jack Daniels sauce, and their smoked pork platter is also a good one. They also serve up country ham, liver and onions, pot roast, and grilled catfish, all with the down-home sides you'd expect, like pinto beans and turnip greens. The atmosphere here is totally casual, with drinks served in Mason jars. Be prepared to wait, however. Everything is home-cooked upon ordering.

Smoky Junction Restaurant (7735 Lamar Alexander Pkwy., 865/448-6881, $3–8) is the place to go for breakfast in Townsend. Not only is it cheap, but the options are seemingly endless. They serve eggs any way you like them accompanied by country ham, bacon, or sausage; you'll find all the other staples like buttermilk pancakes, french toast, omelets, pork chops, and biscuits and gravy—all serious comfort food.

Little River BBQ (8303 Hwy. 73, 865/448-2500, $3–17) offers dining on the river and the same kind of fare you'll find just about everywhere around Townsend—traditional country food, including some very good hand-pulled pork. You can order ribs for two, which comes with three side dishes and bread.

INFORMATION AND SERVICES

The **Townsend Visitor Center** (7906 E. Lamar Alexander Pkwy., 865/448-6134, www.smokymountains.org, daily 9 A.M.–5 P.M.) features both a Great Smoky Mountains Association visitors center and a visitors center for the community of Townsend.

GETTING THERE

If you're coming into Townsend from the west, take I-40 to Exit 386B at Highway 129 south, the same road on which McGhee-Tyson Airport is located. At Maryville, head north on Highway 321, which goes right through Townsend. You might want to do the same if coming from the north (take I-40 to Exit 386B and follow the same directions). While you can certainly exit at Highway 66 and come through Pigeon Forge, the traffic is likely to be heavy, so I still recommend this route for northern visitors.

If you're coming in from Asheville and points east, take I-40 west toward Knoxville, and follow the same route taking Highway 129 south.

From the Atlanta area and points south, you can take I-85 north to Highway 441. Follow 441 to Maryville, and then take 321 north to Townsend.

TENNESSEE FOOTHILLS

MOON SPOTLIGHT
GREAT SMOKY MOUNTAINS
NATIONAL PARK
Avalon Travel
a member of the Perseus Books Group
1700 Fourth Street
Berkeley, CA 94710, USA
www.moon.com

Editor and Series Manager: Kathryn Ettinger
Copy Editor: Amy Scott
Graphics and Production Coordinator:
    Lucie Ericksen
Cover Designer: Kathryn Osgood
Map Editor: Brice Ticen
Cartographer: Kat Bennett

ISBN: 978-1-59880-832-2

Front cover photo: fall in the Great Smoky Mountains
National Park © Jun Ji/Dreamstime.com

Title page photo: © French C. Grimes

* Photo page 8: Maggie-tower-view-nc1.jpg © Bms4880
<http://commons.wikimedia.org/wiki/User:Bms4880>
/http://commons.wikimedia.org
This file is licensed under the Creative Commons
<http://en.wikipedia.org/wiki/en:Creative_Commons>
Attribution 3.0 Unported <http://creativecommons.
org/licenses/by/3.0/deed.en> license.

Printed in the United States

ABOUT THE AUTHOR

Deborah Huso

A mountain girl since birth, Deborah Huso grew up on a small farm in Virginia's Blue Ridge Mountains, just six miles from Shenandoah National Park. Throughout her childhood, she camped, hiked, and explored along the Skyline Drive and Blue Ridge Parkway, developing a love for the southern Appalachian landscape. Deborah left the mountains briefly to study English and history at Gettysburg College, and then to pursue her graduate degree in American studies at The College of William and Mary, but came back to the mountains as soon as she could.

Over the course of the last 10 years, the Smoky Mountains have become a second home to Deborah, who has spent countless hours wandering the region's back roads, hiking trails, and small mountain towns. Her passion is discovering the road less traveled and the trail where you'll meet no one.

Deborah has written more than 100 articles on the Blue Ridge and Smoky Mountains for national and regional magazines and newspapers, including *Women's Health*, *AAA World*, *Disney's FamilyFun*, *Preservation*, *Military Officer*, and *Blue Ridge Country*, where she also serves as contributing editor. To learn more about Deborah, visit her website at www.drhuso.com, or check out her travel blog at www.deborahhuso.com, where she keeps readers updated on the latest news from the Blue Ridge.